Led by Word and Spirit

For no other foundation can any one lay than that which is laid, which is Jesus Christ.
—1 Corinthians 3:11

Led by Word and Spirit

Dale W. Brown

The Brethren Press
Elgin, Illinois

Evangel Press
Nappanee, Indiana

Faith and Life Press
Newton, Kansas

Mennonite Publishing House
Scottdale, Pennsylvania

Scripture quotations, unless otherwise noted, are from the Revised Standard Version of the Bible, copyrighted 1946, 1952, © 1971, 1973.

A publication of The Foundation Series for Adults

Executive Director: Helmut Harder

Published by the Brethren in Christ Church, E. Morris Sider, editor; the Church of the Brethren, June A. Miller, editor; the General Conference Mennonite Church, Elizabeth Yoder, editor; and the Mennonite Church, Levi Miller, editor. Cooperative user: the Mennonite Brethren Church, Dennis Becker, editorial representative.

Designers: David Hiebert, Ken Stanley

Contents

Unit B
Living in the Spirit

The Holy Spirit, sent from God, is a comfort and a guide for believers. As Christians we claim the gifts of the Spirit and through the Spirit's power participate in mission in the world.

Foreword

Is it possible for one book to adequately deal with the themes of Jesus as the Word of God, the authority of Scripture, and the life and work of the Holy Spirit? Even the author of *Led by Word and Spirit* raised the question. And yet, after stating the problem, Dale W. Brown masterfully moved into the task in a way that will help readers consider biblical understandings of the Word and the Spirit and the leading of both Word and Spirit in believers' lives.

It is appropriate that this final book in The Foundation Series for Adults consider these most fundamental faith issues. And we have been well prepared by earlier studies in the series: life in the faith community, the meaning of the Christian faith, living as God's family in the congregation and the home, the kingdom of God, peace and justice, missions and evangelism, discipleship and stewardship. These significant studies have led us well to our present consideration of the Bible as God's word, Jesus Christ as the Word made flesh, and the Holy Spirit as God's living presence in and through believers.

Dale Brown handles well the difficult task of writing about theology and doctrine in ways that speak clearly to the reader's life. Illustrations from his own childhood and growing-up years, examples from his work with seminary students, and stories of individuals and congregations help to "bring home" to the reader the ideas Brown wants to convey. Brown's use of analogies, stories, and humor to convey deep truths about the Christian faith remind one of the master teacher's use of parables.

Writing for five different denominations is not an easy assignment. Yet the author sensitively presents varied understandings and interpretations about the Bible, Jesus the Christ, and the Holy Spirit. His treatment of these issues will bring to readers a new appreciation of both the varieties and the similarities within Anabaptist thought.

The first five chapters of *Led by Word and Spirit* provide a thoughtful study of Jesus Christ as the Word of God made flesh, the very foundation of the church. In considering the authority of the Bible as God's word, Brown presents various understandings of scriptural authority and then looks at the distinctiveness of the Anabaptist position: the place of the Book being in the midst of the gathered community and the task of discerning the word of God being a congregational task. In chapter five Brown considers the relationship between the outer word (the Scriptures) and the inner word (the Holy Spirit) and then affirms that, for Anabaptists, the inner word and the outer word in reality become one: the living word.

"Living in the Spirit," the second unit of this book, is a challenging and joyous consideration of the power and presence of the Holy Spirit in our midst. Careful study of biblical texts, Anabaptist understandings of the Spirit, and the recognition of the Spirit's work in today's world are major themes. Readers are challenged to ask: What does it mean to be "filled with the Spirit"? How do we discover and then use the gifts of the Spirit? How is the Spirit's fruit evidenced in our lives? What does it mean to be sent by the Spirit into the world in mission?

Led by Word and Spirit is a rich addition to The Foundation Series for Adults. (For an outline of the two-year course, see the inside back cover of this book.) Both individuals and congregational groups will be called to consider in new ways the leading of God's Word and God's Spirit in their lives.—June A. Miller, Editor

Introduction

Though I have felt the importance of this study on Word and Spirit, this assignment has often seemed to me to be the epitome of folly. How can anyone write about biblical authority, the doctrine of Christ, and the work of the Holy Spirit in a way which represents five denominations and speaks to their members? Other reservations quickly surfaced. I judged that I might be better qualified to write on church-state issues or a theology of peacemaking. Besides, I had already written a book on the Holy Spirit for my denomination, *Flamed by the Spirit* (Elgin: The Brethren Press, 1978). What more could I say? Also, I felt a bit restricted in working with a structure of chapters and specific topics already devised by the editors.

Nevertheless, the Anabaptist side of me said yes. I have often discovered that when the church lays hands on you, you are led down paths which are more blessed and fruitful than anticipated. It was good for my soul to do basic biblical study on so many specific passages. In areas where I had written before, I discovered there is so much more to learn. I hope that in some ways my experience will be shared as new light breaking forth from the Word.

This has been a good opportunity to become better acquainted with the history and beliefs of sister denominations with whom I have felt close. I have attempted to focus on basic beliefs which come from our common heritage. While not ignoring differences, I have attempted to deal with our differences in ways that do not attack what is cherished in any of our traditions. I know that I have not always succeeded in this, and I assume responsibility for lack of judgment and charity. I do want to thank the editors and readers in the denominational traditions for their help in this sensitive area.

As one who teaches theology in a seminary, I have felt a strong need to put into practice a bit of what I espouse in the classroom. This yearning has drawn me into a bail-fund group and the peace movement. Likewise, I have attempted to relate closely to fellow believers in local congregations. But this desire for the theoretical to become practical does not mean that I have forsaken the importance of sound doctrine. Though I do yearn for the practical, I also believe in the foundational. This writing task has led me to discern anew the importance of clarifying our faith.

In relationship to popular religion and our larger society, it is important that we think through more clearly our views of biblical inspiration and authority. In light of the benefits and pitfalls of the charismatic movements, we need sound biblical study on the doctrine of the Holy Spirit. In terms of evangelism we belong to a tradition which calls each one of us to give a reason for the hope which lies in us. In answer to those who protest that we are to live our faith rather than talk about it, we must remember that talking is basic to living. If we live our religion, we will talk about it and will want to share it with others.

In the spirit of thanksgiving for my own spiritual pilgrimage, I acknowledge my indebtedness to the Mennonites and Quakers. I belong to the Church of the Brethren, which, along with the Brethren in Christ and the Mennonite Brethren, consciously claims both Anabaptist and Pietist rootage. For this reason I have for a long time looked to Mennonite interpreters of the faith for help and inspiration. The more mystical and Spirit-filled orientation of the Quakers has nurtured my Pietist side. This combination of faithfulness to the biblical words and Word, even Jesus Christ, with a sense of expectancy in the leading and power of the Holy Spirit will be the central theme of our study together.

1.
The Word Became Flesh

Scripture Focus: Matthew 12:1-14; Luke 24:44-49; John 1:1-18; 8:58; 1 Corinthians 3:11.

"In the beginning was the Word, and the Word was with God, and the Word was God" (John 1:1). John introduces the fourth gospel with a prologue about *logos*, the Greek word for Word. The practical side of our Anabaptist heritage has often made us suspicious of anything philosophical. When we consider the biblical word *logos*, however, we are forced to admit that it was associated with many theological and philosophical meanings. For the Jews, *logos* pointed to the creative power of God in action; *logos* meant God's self-revelation in power, wisdom, and love. To the Greeks, *logos* was the rational principle which was a part of all reality.

Perhaps John was not as foreign to our bias as we might think. For him all of these philosophical meanings were somehow incorporated in a person. John simplified things: the Word was Jesus Christ. Similarly, Karl Barth, when asked to summarize his thousands of pages of dogma in a few words, replied: "Jesus loves me; this I know because the Bible tells me so."

In this first chapter of *Led by Word and Spirit* we will consider three issues: the centrality of Christ, the Word, for our faith; the personal nature of God's revelation to humankind; and the divinity and humanity of Jesus Christ.

The Centrality of Jesus, the Word

Numerous New Testament passages name this person, Jesus, as the clue to the meaning of life. Paul beholds "the light of knowledge of God in the face of Christ" (2 Cor. 4:6). Also, Paul, who himself was the founder of many churches, asserted that there is "no other foundation . . . than that which is laid, which is Jesus Christ" (1 Cor. 3:11). In the great hymn to Christ, the Philippians are pointed to the "name which is above every name" (2:9). And John, later in his gospel, highlights the primacy of one who claims, "Before Abraham was, I am" (John 8:58).

Jesus himself speaks of his centrality for the meaning of life. The situation is a dispute between the Pharisees and the disciples who had plucked and eaten grain on the sabbath. Jesus appeals to their common heritage: David entered the house of God and ate when hungry; the priests often worked and offered sacrifices on the sabbath. In addition, there was the prophecy of Hosea who declared the wishes of Yahweh: "I desire mercy, and not sacrifice." Yet even as Jesus quotes from the old, he adds that something greater than the temple's laws is involved: "For the Son of man is lord of the sabbath" (Matt. 12:1-8).

Believers' Church people have identified with most of Christendom in centering on Jesus Christ. Menno Simons declared simply, "All the Scriptures, both Old and New Testaments, on every hand, point us to Christ Jesus that we are to follow Him." The names which introduce the stories of the faithful witnesses in the *Martyrs' Mirror* are frequently followed by phrases such as "burnt alive for the name and testimony of Jesus Christ." Church of the Brethren founder Alexander Mack admonished, "Look alone to Jesus your

John 1:1,14

In the beginning was the Word, and the Word was with God, and the Word was God. . . . And the Word became flesh and dwelt among us, full of grace and truth; we have beheld his glory, glory as of the only Son from the Father.

Redeemer and Saviour." This statement is typical of the Christ-centered focus of the Believers' Church family. The inward word quickly comes to be identified with seeking "the mind of Christ" (1 Cor. 2:16; Phil. 2:5).

The Nature of God's Revelation

"And the Word became flesh and dwelt among us, full of grace and truth" (John 1:14). Such a *Christ-centered approach* leads to fairly orthodox views of *the nature of God's revelation.* Revelation simply means God's self-disclosure. How did and how does God get through to us? From our side, how do we know God's nature, ways, and will?

From the beginning, Anabaptists have learned from the prayer life of the spiritualists. But they have rejected extreme expressions of spiritualism which give less importance to the Christ event and more importance to the direct knowledge of God through the Spirit's presence. Anabaptists believe that such direct revelations need to be tested by the disclosure of God we know in Jesus as we learn of his nature in the Scriptures and in the body of believers. In general, Anabaptists have been open to the possibilities of God's self-manifestation through other religions, persons, and activity. But they have insisted that Jesus Christ is the measure whereby people know or do not know that something is from God or is not from God.

In a similar way, the biblical Anabaptists departed from the rationalists of their day. The philosophical view of these people saw the mind as the image of God in each person. Since God created the universe to be orderly and rational, persons know best through reason. Thus, through reason people grow in understanding God's truth and laws. But the Anabaptist view insists that the disclosure which became flesh and dwelt among us was full of grace as well as truth. This does not mean that conceptual truth and laws are eliminated. They must, however, be related to love. When the gospel writer refers to the truth which sets us free, he is pointing to a person, to a personal relationship. In the Bible, truth is more than conceptual, stating ideas about God; it is relational, knowing God as a person.

Many popular efforts to know God through our own

minds, intuition, mystical experiences, or moral behavior carry the spirit of the little girl who was absorbed in drawing a picture. When asked what she was drawing, she replied, "I am making a picture of God." Her questioner protested, "But no one knows what God looks like." Quickly, she responded, "They will when I get through." The good news of the Christian message is not that we can easily manage God; the good news is that God came to us. We cannot make God in our image. For God's ways and thoughts are higher than our ways and thoughts (Isa. 55:8-9). Because God came to us, the Believers' Church tradition has insisted that faith means a wholehearted response to God's action. Faith expresses itself in joy; faith seeks to understand the message; faith becomes active in love.

Some seekers, such as the Muslims, give a book priority over their prophet. Others choose an institution—the church, the lodge, the nation—as the object of supreme allegiance around which they find meaning and purpose for living.

Though some of these objects of faith—such as the Bible, the church, and prayer—are basic to what we name as Christian, ours is not primarily a religion based on an infallible book or institution, on moral codes, or on mystical ladders. Rather, Christianity is a religion centered on a person. In a real sense this remains a mystery and a stumbling block. We can never be completely in control when the revelation is personal. God remains, in a sense, hidden in Christ. We "know in part . . . our knowledge is imperfect . . . we see in a mirror dimly" (1 Cor. 13).

Yet, in another sense, there is logic in the way Christians believe God acted. If God really wanted to get through to persons, what better way to do it than to become a person? It has been well stated that when God placed a call to the human race, it was not station-to-station but person-to-person. And because the Christian faith proclaims that God spoke through a person, we know a personal God. In biblical thought, to know means more than to think abstractly; it means to think and to relate intimately. And since God's nature is unveiled and found to be a person, our heritage leads us to proclaim the dignity and worth of each and every person.

14

Jesus, Both Divine and Human

"And the Word became flesh and dwelt among us . . ." (John 1:14). Issues arising from faith in the *centrality of Christ* and the *personal nature of revelation* have been less divisive than questions about the *nature of the person of Jesus Christ*. Ancient creeds declared Jesus to be true God of true God yet one who for our sakes came down from the heavens and was made flesh. But how can one person be both divine and human? And which of these two should be the focus of our message?

Literally, the Johannine text says that God pitched a tent to dwell with us. Such an affirmation was scandalous to a popular group of that day, the Gnostics. As intellectuals, they believed they had special knowledge about a way to God through intermediaries and angelic beings. They pictured a ladder of ascent and descent between people and God. They saw Jesus as being the greatest of these intermediaries, but they refused to place him at the top on a level with God. And they would not grant that he belonged so far down the ladder as to be like humans.

Many Gnostics held to Docetism, a belief that Jesus' body was in reality a spiritual body which just appeared to be human. Some Gnostics concluded that a spiritual body could not possibly have been nailed to a cross. According to one theory, the crucifiers were deceived; they nailed to

15

the cross the body of Simon of Cyrene, who, when compelled to carry the cross, had traded places with Jesus.

The author of the Gospel of John spoke to the reluctance to place Jesus at the top. John located the origin of Jesus in the activity of God in creation. He also opposed the docetic views which would not allow Jesus to be fully human. John claimed that in Christ, God had become fully human, or flesh. John's references to Jesus' physical and emotional attributes are further teachings against the views of the Gnostics.

In his prologue John identified the Word with both the grandeur of God's work in creation and with one historical time, place, and person. Christ is both the preexistent creator and the crucified one. Contrary to the Gnostics, who gave an intermediary place to Jesus, John places Jesus both on a level equal with God and on a lower level with humanity.

Early Anabaptist leaders were not unified in their beliefs about the human and divine nature of Christ. Agreeing with Dirk Phillips, Menno Simons found it difficult to think of Jesus as completely human. He reasoned that Mary did not give Jesus her flesh and blood. This refusal to grant resemblance between the first Adam and the new Adam (Christ) may have been related to Menno's desire that the church, Christ's body, be holy and without blemish, in contrast to the state churches. More representative of Anabaptism on this issue, however, was the confession of faith of Ambrosius Spittelmayr (1527): "Christ, true God and true man, the head of all His members."

At a Believers' Church gathering at Bluffton College in the fall of 1980, I was impressed that the Mennonites did not feel it necessary to defend Menno's views on the nature of the person of Christ. In the Anabaptist tradition the community consensus is more important than the views of any one leader. And being open to new light as it breaks forth from the word of God means that we are free from making absolute the teachings of the founders.

At this conference John Howard Yoder suggested how the biblical view of the two natures of Christ has been helpful to our tradition. Only if Christ embodies more than all of our best wisdom, only if his call is grounded in the

16

biblical Word, does it challenge our conformity to our own age. Only if the Lamb which was slain is worthy because he was slain to redeem the world, is there any motivation for martyrs to take up the cross of Jesus.

Similarly, Yoder drew lessons for our tradition from a focus on the humanity of our Lord. Only if Jesus is fully human, can the Way become imaginable for his disciples. Christ can only be Savior if we can identify with one who was fully human and tempted in every way as we. At the same time, Christ can only be Savior if he is different enough to pull us toward the vision of what life should be.

I once knew a student who struggled for months with this issue of Jesus' humanity and divinity. One day he would come into my office saying that only if Jesus is not like me, can he save me from what I am. And on another day he would exclaim that only if Jesus is completely like me, can I ever have any hope of being like him.

Today scholars deal with the issue by talking about "Christology from above" and "Christology from below." Christology from above begins with the divinity of Christ and moves on to include the significance of the man who died on a cross. Christology from below begins with the man, Jesus, and moves to see how that life was somehow divine.

The Believers' Churches have affirmed both the divinity and the humanity of Christ. In their insistence on the humanity of Jesus, they have brought a needed corrective to traditions which focus almost entirely on the divine nature of Christ. These Reformation radicals called the world to "behold the man." The Believers' Churches have regarded the life and teachings of Jesus as being as important as his death and resurrection. The meaning of Christ's death cannot properly be understood apart from the quality of the life he gave up. A golden text has been 1 Peter 2:21: "For to this you have been called, because Christ also suffered for you, leaving you an example, that you should follow in his steps."

An Episcopal student enrolled in the Brethren college where I taught in Kansas. After several weeks he appeared in my office with a puzzled look on his face. He said that he had grown up hearing about Christ and Jesus Christ but never had he been in a place where there was so much talk about Jesus! Why all of this Jesus talk? The Jesus language comes from both Anabaptism and Pietism. It points to the medieval piety which lay behind the *imitatio* (imitation of Christ) emphasis. Bernard of Clairveaux, writing in the twelfth century, expressed a Jesus mysticism which Francis of Assisi lived out in the next century. This mysticism hallowed daily life instead of attempting to escape from life. In this Jesus mysticism the believer strives to identify with the Way and the love of Jesus.

We who belong to the Believers' Church tradition, however, do need to be careful that our focus on Jesus' humanity not overshadow his divinity. A Reformed brother, speaking at the same Believers' Church meeting referred to earlier, appealed to us at this very point. He felt that we must not neglect the adoration which comes from a focus on Christ's divinity. Along with our emphasis on the call to follow Jesus, we also need the message of the divine Savior who forgives us when we fail to live out our call.

Our tradition at its best calls us to proclaim Christ as both Lord and Savior. Although we have been reluctant to adopt creeds, we can join the chorus of those who confess "very God of very God *and* very man of very man."

A Believers' Church Sermon

What is God like? People brought little children—noisy, dirty, unruly little creatures—to Jesus. His disciples did not wish their Master to be bothered by such persons at the close of a very busy day. But Jesus said, "Let the children come to me, and do not hinder them, for to such belongs the kingdom of heaven" (Matt. 19:14). Christians believe that God is like that.

What is God like? The disciples were plucking grain and eating it as they walked through the fields on the sabbath. This was in direct violation of the customs of the day and the laws of strict religion. The religious leaders protested to Jesus. He replied, "The sabbath was made for man, not man for the sabbath" (Mark 2:27). Christians believe that God is like that.

What is God like? It was a great religious feast day in Jerusalem. People had traveled great distances to make their sacrifices at the temple. They needed to exchange

Bob Taylor

their money; they had to purchase offerings of animals and goods. Certain people were taking advantage of the situation. Jesus was angry about this injustice. He tipped over the tables of the money-changers and the seats of those who sold pigeons. He quoted the prophets: "It is written, 'My house shall be called a house of prayer'; but you make it a den of robbers" (Matt. 21:13). Christians believe that God is like that.

What is God like? The disciples were gathering for their last meal together. In a dramatic action, Jesus arose from the table and assumed the role of the lowliest of servants. He began to wash the disciples' feet. Over their protests, he lived out what he taught: The greatest must become the servant of all. Christians believe that God is like that.

What is God like? Jesus' last trip out of Jerusalem was to a hill, Calvary. He was dragged. They scourged him, mocked him, spit on him, nailed him to a cross, and pierced him in the side. In the midst of the most unjust trial and punishment of all time, Jesus prayed for those who were killing him: "Father, forgive them; for they know not what they do" (Luke 23:34). Christians believe that God is like that.

What is God like? Christians believe that God is like Jesus, the Christ. "For it is the God who said, 'Let light shine out of darkness,' who has shone in our hearts to give the light of the knowledge of the glory of God in the face of Christ" (2 Cor. 4:6).

2.
Authority in Faith and Life

Scripture Focus: Joshua 1:8; Matthew 5:17-21; 2 Timothy 3:14—4:5.

"May the Lord add his blessing to the reading of his Holy Word!" Spoken reverently and devoutly, such words point to what is basic in the Believers' Church tradition. The Bible is assumed to be God's Word. The Anabaptists, yesterday and today, have aspired to be "people of the book." "Do not depend upon men," cried Menno; "put your trust in Christ alone and his word." In early confessions of faith, Anabaptists took the matter of biblical inspiration and authority for granted. Early records in town archives reveal that brothers and sisters who were brought before the courts possessed an amazing knowledge of the Scriptures. The evidence clearly suggests that our tradition has known a strong consensus in identifying the Word of God with the Bible.

Understanding the Bible as the Word
Anabaptists have not always agreed about the Word. Though nearly all were biblicists in that they relied greatly on the Bible, an early difference centered on the interpretation of the Word. Hans Denck, a spiritualist Anabaptist leader, was perhaps the most vocal in his refusal to identify the Scriptures with the Word: "I value the scriptures above all earthly treasures, but not so highly as the word of God." According to Denck, Hans Hut, and others, the Scriptures are not the wine but the sign outside the inn which advertises the wine.

Though such opinions have been said to be on the fringes of the Anabaptist movement, we can learn something from them. Christians have not always escaped bibliolatry, which is the worship of the Bible as a book in a way that overshadows the gospel message. Such bibliolatry may be the very concern found at the end of the fifth chapter of John: "You search the scriptures," Jesus admonished, "because you think that in them you have eternal life; and it is they that bear witness to me; yet you refuse to come to me that you may have life."

Martin Luther, the father of the Protestant Reformation, insisted that Christ, or the gospel, is truly the Word. The Bible, according to Luther, is the manger, or cradle, in which the Word, Christ, is laid. The law and prophets are the swaddling clothes in which Christ is wrapped. From this imagery of Luther's, some persons have reasoned that the Bible is not the Word of God but that the Bible contains the Word of God.

But this way of stating it has problems. Luther himself struggled with the issue. He popularized the slogan, *sola scriptura,* scripture alone; he spoke of the living Word, Jesus Christ, coming to us as the spoken word, the visible word, and the written word. In taking a lead from Luther, many persons have moved one step further, declaring that the Word, Christ, can become the living Word for us through a sermon, through participation in the Lord's supper, or through meditation on a scriptural passage. Such formulations do keep alive the idea of the primacy of Christ as the Word. They focus on the dynamic nature of Christ, the Word, coming alive in the hearts of believers.

Psalm 119:105
> *Thy word is a lamp to my feet*
> *and a light to my path.*

1 Thessalonians 2:13
> *And we also thank God constantly for this, that when you received the word of God which you heard from us, you accepted it not as the word of men but as what it really is, the word of God, which is at work in you believers.*

But there may be more helpful ways of talking about the Bible as the Word. The Bible may be compared to an undeveloped negative. What it really is, the Word of God, becomes apparent when it is exposed by the light of the Holy Spirit in the context of the community of faith. This suggests that the truth of Scripture is there from the moment God inspired it. When, under the Spirit's guidance, we are led to see that truth, we merely discover what was true all along. The Word, with its objective reality and intrinsic authority, precedes our moment of illumination concerning it. Christ, through the Bible, remains knocking at the door whether we open it or not.

The Witness of the Bible Itself

More important and helpful than either the views of Hans Denck or Martin Luther are the views of the biblical writers themselves. How do they speak to the issues before us? The Church of the Brethren spent several years seeking guidance and unity on questions of biblical authority. The following statements are quoted directly from that study and speak clearly to the issue we are considering (from the section "The Witness of the Bible Itself," in the "Biblical Inspiration and Authority, 1979 Annual Conference Paper").

. . . Not only in isolated texts, but in currents and undercurrents of its larger message, the Bible supplies a helpful framework for thinking about inspiration and authority.

(1) *God speaks!* The picture of God speaking the word is central to the Bible. Far from being a silent God remote from the affairs of life, God continually speaks of mercy and judgment. Thus it is that scripture is replete with references to "the word of the Lord," "the word of God," and related expressions. (Isaiah 55:11, Amos 3:7, Hebrews 4:12-13).

(2) *God speaks to us to create a covenant with us.* . . . The Bible does not present God as one who utters timeless truths to satisfy the speculative interest of theologians. Rather, God speaks in order to draw us into a covenant of steadfast love.

At the very beginning of God's relationship with

Bob Taylor

Israel, God invites Israel to enter into a covenant and commissions Moses to set forth the "words" which make up that covenant (Exodus 19:5-6, 24:7, 34:27-38). . . . Whether through stone tablets, books, or "living letters" (2 Corinthians 3:1-6), God speaks to us as our covenant partner.

(3) *God's Spirit equips us to speak God's word to one another.* The voices through which God speaks are human voices. Though we are inclined to set "divine" and "human" in opposition to each other, the biblical writers do not. (Ezekiel 2:1-2, Joel 2:28-29, Luke 1:2, John 16:12-15, Acts 1:8, Acts 2:17-18, 1 Peter 2:10-12). Through the words that these persons speak, God's own word is made known to God's people.

(4) *Words spoken for God in the past have a continuing life among God's people.* . . . So it is that Jeremiah appeals to the Mosaic covenant in his prophetic ministry in Jerusalem (Jeremiah 11:1-8). So it is that the story of the exodus through the wilderness gives rise to a hope in a new exodus for a people in exile (Isaiah 41:17-20; 42:16-21). So it is that the early church drew on the promises of the prophets to discern the meaning of Jesus' life (Acts 8:30-35).

(5) *Different ways of speaking for God may be necessary in different generations.* . . . Jeremiah, for example, rejects the false hopes of those who used Isaiah's promise of Jerusalem's security as a basis for moral complacency (cf. Isaiah 31:4-5; Jeremiah 7:1-15). Jesus challenges the finality of certain parts of the law of Moses (Mark 10:1-12; Matthew 5:21-48). . . . And James takes issue with those who misused Paul's language about justification by faith alone (James 2:14-26).

(6) *Scripture sets forth God's word with power and authority.* Because those who speak for God in the biblical account were guided by the Holy Spirit, all scripture is attested as "inspired of God" or "God-breathed" (2 Timothy 3:16). The Bible is thus not only a great work of literature, but a canon of faith and life for the community of believers.

So it is that the psalmist can extol the words of the

law as a lamp to our feet and a light to our path (Psalm 119:105). So it is that scripture can be acclaimed as "profitable for teaching, for reproof, for correction, and for training in righteousness" (2 Timothy 3:16). So it is that Paul can call the apostolic message the word of God, and not merely a human word (1 Thessalonians 2:13). So it is that Jesus affirms in the Fourth Gospel that "scripture cannot be broken" (John 10:35).

(7) *Jesus Christ expresses God's word in a complete and decisive way.* . . . Though we are constantly discovering new ways to speak God's word, God's self-disclosure in Jesus now sets the ground rules for this language.

In many and varied ways the New Testament affirms this centrality of Jesus . . . all who would speak God's word now must speak in the light of God's word in and through Jesus.

(8) *God calls us to become a faithful community of the word.* . . . Though the biblical writers never call us to believe in scripture for its own sake, they summon the church in various ways to live out of the message which the scriptures proclaim.

Jesus himself supplies the model for the faithful church. Jesus values and respects the Old Testament as a resource for his teaching ministry (Matthew 21:33-46; Mark 12:18-37; Luke 11:29-32). He defines his own mission in terms of a scriptural hope in the day of salvation for the afflicted and oppressed (Luke 4:18-19). . . . And he appeals to scripture in various ways to bring his hearers to understanding and decision (Matthew 11:20-24; Mark 2:23-28; 10:2-9).

So too we are to guard and follow the truth that has been entrusted to us by the Holy Spirit (2 Timothy 1:13-14). We are to give first importance to the message which was of first importance to the early church (1 Corinthians 15:1-5). We are to guard against twisting God's word with our private misinterpretations (2 Peter 1:20). We are to allow scripture to serve its intended purpose of leading others to life in Christ (John 5:39-40). We are to handle the word of God with integrity and openness . . . (2 Corinthians 4:1-2). And we are to declare anew the wonderful deeds of God who called us out of darkness into light (1 Peter 2:9).

Anabaptist-Brethren Views About the Bible

The following paragraphs represent an attempt to summarize the stance of five denominations toward the "Book of Books." All of these church bodies in one way or another trace their origins back to the first Anabaptists, who called each other Brethren. And the three who have used the word Brethren in their official denominational name also have strong Pietist roots. Such variety complicates the task. But I am convinced that we share so much in common that our variety is encompassed in a larger tradition. In the spirit of that tradition I offer this outline, not as a creed or even a proposed statement of faith but for our mutual study and discussion.

1. Mind of Christ

Our heritage has suggested that the Bible is not an end in itself but that it leads us to Christ. In countless texts, such as the passage in Matthew 5:17-20, Jesus is proclaimed as the fulfillment of the law. What is promised in the Scriptures is fulfilled in Jesus. However, this can also work in the opposite direction. The Scriptures should be approached through Jesus Christ. The Old Mennonite Confession of Faith adopted by their General Conference in 1963 puts it well: "Jesus is the key to the proper understanding of the entire Bible." A popular variation of this principle has circulated in some of our circles: The Old Testament must be interpreted in the light of the New Testament and both of these must be interpreted by the mind of Christ. A Jesus mysticism, flowing from Pietist sources, has assumed that saturation and identification with the love of Jesus will help people to understand the sacred writings.

2. The Inner Word and the Outer Word

Early Anabaptists found themselves between those who held firmly to the outer Word (the Scriptures) and those who relied almost entirely on the inner Word (the Holy Spirit). They emphasized both an obedience to the outer Word and a receptivity to the working of the Holy Spirit.

They refused to separate the inner Word from the outer Word. They saw the life-giving Spirit of God illuminating the written and the inspired Word of God. In this way they avoided a dead legalism on the one hand and a formless inspirationalism on the other.

3. Gathering Around the Word

The Bible is best understood as the community of faith gathers around the Word. This constitutes what has been named the Anabaptist hermeneutic (principle of biblical interpretation). The locus of authority is not in the text itself or in the highly qualified theological expert. Rather the locus of authority is found in the text encountering the committed, believing congregation. The unique authority of the revelation of God in Christ which is found in the Bible becomes apparent in the covenant relationships of the responding community. This style of interpretation often sees a shift from the "I language" of most of Protestantism to the "we language" which the Bible itself uses. At the same time, Pietist influences among us insist that personal faith must both contribute to and be nurtured by corporate discernment.

4. Priority of the New Testament

Though not all of our church bodies have adopted the Dunker slogan, "No creed but the New Testament," there is a consensus among our churches that higher authority is given to the New Testament. Nineteenth-century Levi Lukenbach's report about the founders of the Brethren in Christ represents this stance. He noted the founders' determination to reject all creeds and to stand upon the authority of Scripture, with special attention, however, to the New Testament as the highest level of God's self-revelation.

In examining the Sermon on the Mount (Matt. 5:17-20) and the examples which follow, two things are clearly seen. First, Jesus was no rebel against the Jewish heritage. He did not come to destroy the law and the prophets, the heart of the Old Testament message. Not the smallest letter, the iota, or dot, will pass from the law until all is accomplished. Second, we must note that Jesus boldly followed his admonition "You have heard that it was said to men of old"

with "But I say to you . . ." It is necessary to proclaim both the continuity and the discontinuity between the Testaments. The Bible gives evidence of a fundamental unity, and yet, at the same time, it is marked by rich diversity and great pluralism. The same great themes continue through the Bible as it tells the story of God's redemptive activity. At the same time, however, Jesus speaks of the significance of his life and suffering as "a new testament, or covenant" (Mark 14:24).

The key to both discontinuity and continuity may be found in Jesus' statement that he came not to destroy but to fulfill the law. The law was fulfilled in Jesus' doing what the law had announced. It was fulfilled as he taught its deeper intent, which concerned the motivation of the doers. Jesus called for a higher righteousness in which the golden rule of love was equated with the whole law and teachings of the prophets (Matt. 7:12). He taught that the whole law can be contained in the love commandments (Matt. 22:40). Jesus placed people above rules, mercy above sacrifices, and spiritual obedience before mechanical obedience. These teachings of Jesus, however, had also been a part of the prophet's message. Therefore, the new freedom to be found in living the law would not abolish the law as much as fulfill it.

Many Arab Christians have developed an antipathy toward the Old Testament because it has been misused to support contemporary claims to land. Generally, however, Christians have rejected the ancient Marcionite heresy, which rejected the Old Testament because its message offered a God of wrath instead of the God of love found in Christianity. Christians have preferred the advice that "all scripture is inspired by God and profitable for teaching" (2 Tim. 3:16). We cannot properly understand the message of the New Testament apart from understanding the foundation on which it stands. The New Testament writers drew heavily from certain sections of the Old Testament as a way to present the heart of the Christian gospel.

Most Christians, however, find some problems in relating and differentiating between the Testaments. Generally, Christians have agreed with Calvin's conclusion that the ceremonial law of the Old Testament has been displaced by the new covenant. Thus, most Christians no longer observe the food regulations, the strictures against shaving, the seventh-day sabbath, and animal sacrifices. Though Calvin taught that the ceremonial law had been displaced, he also taught that the moral law should be observed. In Calvin's Geneva the Leviticus statutes dealing with adultery and homosexuality were kept, and children who cursed their parents were put to death as commanded in Leviticus 20:9. Most Christians today, however, read such a command in light of the larger message of the Bible.

It is impossible to understand our stance on this question apart from the situation of the early Anabaptists. The Reformers drew heavily on the Old Testament to support death sentences for our ancestors in the faith. They found support there for persecution by the state church, the continuity of infant baptism from Jewish circumcision, and the denial of religious freedom. On the other side, the Anabaptists' ability to differentiate between the two covenants supported their two most distinctive ethical emphases: nonswearing and the refusal to participate in bloodshed. Though both had been permitted in the Old Testament, the Anabaptists found that the New Testament message showed a better way. Although they did not grant the Old Testament final authority, the Anabaptists did not reject it. They quoted it profusely. They viewed it as the groundwork on which the building itself rested. They saw the relationship between Old Testament and New Testament Scripture as that of promise and fulfillment.

5. Authority for Faith and Life

Though our five denominations are together in the high authority granted to the Bible, they do have different understandings about the inspiration of the Bible. Most would accept the concept of *verbal* inspiration if this means that the reliability of the Bible extends to words as well as meanings. Many would not agree if the word verbal implies a dictation theory of inspiration in which God mechanically guided the hands of the writers. There would be widespread acceptance of a *plenary* view of inspiration, which simply means that all Scripture is inspired. But some would reject this view if it is used to suggest that all Scripture is equally rich in spiritual content.

The question of inerrancy was not a concern for our mothers and fathers in the faith. This debate over whether the Bible is without factual or historical errors of any kind primarily appears on this side of the scientific revolution, which is so preoccupied with facts and accuracy. The early Anabaptists, however, were quite willing to use the word *infallible* in referring to the Bible. For them this word pointed to the reliability of the Bible as the norm for doctrinal and moral decisions.

For the most part our traditions have been more concerned with the beliefs *of* the Bible than with beliefs *about* the Bible. The biblicism has been practical more than

31

propositional. If one examined the much-read Bible of a Calvinist grandmother, passages such as Romans 1—8 might be worn, wrinkly, and scribbled. On the other hand, if one looked at the much-used Bible of a Mennonite sister, there is a greater chance that Romans 1—8 might be fairly clean. The worn, wrinkly, and scribbled texts would be Romans 12 and Matthew 5—7. J. C. Wenger, who has examined this question extensively, offers a statement which might be a strong, if not universal, consensus among our denominations: "The Bible was written by holy men of God who were born of the Holy Spirit so effectively that all Scripture is 'God-given' and therefore normative for faith and life" (*God's Word Written,* p. 52). The General Conference Mennonite Church statement approved in 1941 may be as representative as any of our belief: "We believe in the divine inspiration and infallibility of the Bible as the Word of God and the only trustworthy guide of faith and life."

If we are faithful to our heritage, we will refuse to injure or violate one another in struggling about a Book which commands us to love one another. The Book will survive. It may not need our defense as much as we might think. In this spirit I like the summary found in the *Gospel Messenger* (Church of the Brethren editorial in 1919): "Straight-forward preaching of scriptural truth, reinforced by a lot of Christian living, is the best defense of the Bible that has ever been devised. . . . Practice will do more than proof to protect it from discredit."

3.
The Community Gathering Around the Word

Scripture Focus: Joshua 1:1-19; Psalm 119:105; 2 Timothy 3:14—4:5; 2 Peter 1:16-21.

"Jesus Christ is the supreme gift given to us in the wrapping of the Bible." This statement from one of my teachers resembles Luther's oft-quoted metaphor: "The Bible is the manger in which Christ is laid." Rather than explore why some people dislike smelly mangers, however, it may be more helpful to focus on the wrapping.

The Wrapping and the Gift
The wrapping, the Bible, evokes a variety of responses. Some contemporaries have not liked the bloodshed, the cosmology (the three-story universe), and the superstitions which provide the framework for the biblical stories. References to the "four corners of the earth" mistakenly assume that our planet is flat. Other persons object to what they regard as X-rated material, such as the sexual transgressions of David. Young intellectuals are often scandalized by minor contradictions, such as Matthew's attributing the "thirty pieces of silver" to Jeremiah instead of Zechariah. Some college students in their first serious attempt to study the Bible become disillusioned when they encounter such critical problems. The great danger for them, as well as for others, is that in rejecting the wrapping they may toss out the package which contains the gift.

Other persons look at the wrapping in an entirely different way. They are tempted to worship the wrapping. Sometimes they seem to resemble children who become so allured by the wrapping that they cannot distinguish between the package and the gift. For many of us, the memories of those who carried, read, and opened the Book for us are so precious that we object to any new wrapping. Such an attitude may help explain the actions of those who burn new editions of the Bible because they want to defend the Bible as it came to them.

The packaging of the Bible, however, has been unlike the holy book of the Muslims. Muslims believe that the Koran was dictated directly by the angel Gabriel to the prophet Mohammed. In principle, therefore, it cannot be translated from the Arabic and still be the Koran. The Christian Bible, however, has been translated into hundreds of languages and versions in order to enable more people to receive the gift, Christ.

Both of the errors described above work against the receiving of the gift. Throwing away the package will result in the loss of the gift. Worshiping the wrapping will keep us from opening the package to receive the gift.

Our heritage, however, brings another observation, as you have probably already guessed. Unwrapping gifts is an event which we share with others. Even when a gift is unwrapped alone, the significance is tied to the fact that it has been given by another, and we are usually most anxious to share with others the good news of the gift. In a similar way, we gather around the Bible to open it in order to discern the meaning of the gift for our lives.

2 Peter 1:20-21
First of all you must understand this, that no prophecy of scripture is a matter of one's own interpretation, because no prophecy ever came by the impulse of man, but men moved by the Holy Spirit spoke from God.

Rightly Dividing the Word of Truth

Each time I entered an institution of higher learning, my mother took me aside to express her deep concern as to what this venture might do to my faith. I have never been able to successfully shake off her concern. I still am open to those who worry about what I, a teacher of preachers, may be doing to the faith of future preachers.

A brother confronted me concerning my bad influence on his son: "You are teaching Barth, Brunner, Bonhoeffer—all theologians—instead of the Bible!" As we were about to part, he gave me several tracts to read. Quickly looking them over, I called him back: "Brother," I said, "we may not be as far apart as I thought. You had me believing that I read theologians and you use only the Bible. But you did not give me printouts of the Scriptures. Rather, you handed me interpretations of the Scriptures by the pastor of your tabernacle. We both have theologians. We both read the Bible. We believe our theologians help us to understand the Word of God more clearly. Our only difference is that we have different theologians."

Thus, we recognize that the Bible comes alive for us as we gather with and learn from others. But then the question comes, With whom do we gather? The Bible can be interpreted in so many different ways. Whom do we trust to "rightly divide the word of truth"?

The problem of whom the community trusts and how the Book is regarded and interpreted has been with the church from the beginning. The relationship between the community and the Bible has been manifested in many different ways. We will look at some of the different ways in which the Bible has been interpreted throughout history and then consider how our heritage has approached this issue.

The People of Israel

The Ten Commandments in Exodus 20 form an early summary of the obligations which bound Israel to God. These pronouncements form part of a treaty or covenant between God and the people. Exodus 24:3-8 describes a ceremony for ratifying this covenant. The ceremony depicts one of the ways in which the Bible came to us. Community declarations about the covenant, the promises

35

and agreements between God and the people, were written down, renewed, revised, expanded, and collated.

These written laws were held in high regard. We see evidence of this in the prologue to the book of Joshua (Josh. 1:1-18). Instructing the one who was to lead the people into the promised land, the Lord said to Joshua, ''This book of the law shall not depart out of your mouth, but you shall meditate on it day and night, that you may be careful to do according to all that is written in it'' (v. 8). This section of the Deuteronomic materials was probably gathered and written many years later, around the seventh century before Christ to encourage the Jews to remain faithful in times of duress.

In the Psalms we also see evidence of the high regard given to these laws. The Psalms are full of poetic affirmations which praise the written law as precious treasure, source of joy and delight, goal of all knowledge, root of enlightenment, standard of conduct, and object of love. One of the countless such expressions is found in Psalm 119:105: "Thy word is a lamp to my feet and a light to my path."

Early Christian

Though the Sadducees limited their authoritative scriptures to the Law, the first five books of the Old Testament, most of the Jews at that time included the Law, the Prophets, and the Writings as their scripture. The early Christians followed this Jewish majority, keeping as their scripture, the Law, the Prophets, and the Writings as translated into Greek. Paul began to write letters of encouragement and advice to new house churches which he had started or visited. Luke desired to write an orderly account of the life, death, and resurrection of Jesus (Luke 1:1-4). From the island of Patmos, an exiled pastoral leader named John wrote a message of hope to the churches in Asia Minor (Revelation). He urged the persecuted to remain faithful, holding on to the spirit of confidence in God's final victory over the forces of evil. These writings are all examples of the beginning of the New Testament.

Still the early church thrived and witnessed faithfully for several generations without the New Testament as we know it. By the end of the second century a book was recognized as canonical when it was read in worship services. Certain books, however, were disputed for centuries. As early as A.D. 367, Athanasius suggested a list of twenty-seven books, which correspond to our present New Testament.

The need for a canon, which means rule of faith, emerged as the church grew larger, encompassed many cultures and peoples, and became divided doctrinally. For the sake of unity, the church moved toward more officially chosen leadership, creedal statements, and a new canon, or rule of faith, to be added to the old covenant. One crucial test for whether a book made it into the canon was whether its message reflected the life and message of one of the apostles who was close to Jesus. At the end of the fourth century, councils formally adopted our present rule of faith and practice, the twenty-seven books we know as the New Testament.

Eastern Orthodox

In the ancient tradition of the Orthodox churches the authority of the Bible cannot be separated from the high view of the church. In Orthodox worship the Bible is venerated as a verbal icon (image) of Christ. In every church it has a place of honor. The faithful kiss the Bible and prostrate themselves before it. Russian Christians quickly point out that they venerate and highly regard the Bible but do not worship it. For people who could not read the Bible at home, whose tradition was thousands of years of illiteracy, the visual image of the Bible, of the priest taking it up and reading from it, was essential. The Bible was the book of the gathering of people in worship. Consequently, it must never be set up over the church or used against the church.

The apostolic tradition of the church is not only older than the New Testament; it is also the source of the New Testament. Holy Scripture is one special form of this apostolic tradition. The creeds and major decisions of the seven ecumenical councils are highly regarded forms of the same tradition. For this reason personal interpretations of the Bible are not to be trusted. They must be placed under the guidance of the church. Each new convert promises, "I will accept and understand Holy Scripture in accordance with the interpretation which was and is held by the Holy Orthodox Catholic Church of the East, our Mother."

Roman Catholic

There are no stronger affirmations of scriptural infallibility than the official pronouncements of Roman Catholicism. The Roman Catholic Bible includes the Apocrypha (a group of books not included in most Protestant Bibles). It is interesting to note that Menno Simons, who was formerly a priest, and other early Anabaptist

38

leaders quoted freely from the Apocrypha.

Catholicism differs from Protestantism not so much in the authority given to the Bible as in the source of that authority. Protestants generally hold the authority to be part of the nature of the Bible itself. Like the Eastern Church, Roman Catholics believe that the authority is derived from the church. Since the church created the Scriptures in the first place, the church remains the infallible interpreter of the Bible. Unity can be preserved through the authoritative interpretations of the pope and the hierarchy.

Roman Catholics saw Protestantism as destroying the unity of Europe through nationalism and individualism. The seamless robe of Christ had been torn. They felt that the church would become splintered if each and every person interpreted the Bible according to his or her whims. Thus, the decision of the Council of Toulouse in 1229 prohibited the laity from possessing Bibles in the vernacular, the national tongue of the people.

This decision has been radically altered in the twentieth century. Since Vatican II the Roman Catholic church has known a genuine biblical revival which has been characterized by intensive biblical study among both scholars and laity. This revival of Bible study points to the unity Roman Catholics believe exists between the living word (the tradition) and the written word (the Bible).

Reformation

In the thick of his disputes with Rome, Luther declared that Scripture alone was the source of Christian truth. Because of this, many people are shocked to learn that Luther seemingly played fast and loose with the Scriptures. He made critical judgments as to whether Moses had written all of the Pentateuch or whether Chronicles was as reliable as Kings. His honest temperament led him to suggest that he wished Esther and Revelation could be eliminated from the canon. Nevertheless, he did share responsibility for making the authority of the Bible one of the central planks of Reformation faith.

Calvin gave the Bible a clearer and more authoritative status than Luther. According to Calvin, the Scriptures ought to have for believers the same authority as if the message were spoken by God directly. Such an emphasis, along with Calvin's stress on the continuity of the moral law of the Old Testament with the New, placed the Bible at the center of Protestant life. In the cathedral at Geneva, statues, altars, the pipe organ, and other symbols of worship were removed. Only the pulpit remained, and on it the Bible was placed. From it the minister read and interpreted the Word of God.

With Luther, Calvin believed that the primary work of the Spirit was to validate, bring alive, and unify our interpretations of the Bible. Calvin's doctrine of the internal testimony of the Holy Spirit was the answer to the Roman Catholic charge that Protestantism would lead to the worst kind of pluralism. The Holy Spirit would maintain unity about what the Bible says.

Time has shown that the Roman Catholics were quite accurate in their prophecies. The Protestant generations which followed the mainline Reformers did splinter into many groups. Within Lutheranism, theologians attempted to resolve dozens of controversies which arose from different interpretations of what Luther had said. Extensive formulations were developed to try to resolve the many conflicts. These were collected, signed by secular and ecclesiastical officials, and officially approved as the Formula of Concord, the collection of creeds known as the Symbolical Books of Lutheranism. The manner in which these creeds were interpreted, debated, and forced upon people fostered the opposition of the Pietists. They questioned using the Bible to find proof-texts to support the creeds rather than studying the Bible for guidance in matters of faith and life.

The Way of Our Heritage

Now to simplify the debate. The Roman Catholics claimed that since the church gathered and approved the canon, the church should remain the guardian and final interpreter. The Protestant leaders answered that Jesus and the witness of those who had been closest to him had created the church in the first place. Further they said that this witness, which is now the New Testament, should remain the infallible authority in the life of the church.

The Anabaptists sensed the interrelatedness of these

two positions. The Book of the people and the people cannot be neatly divided into two separate sources of authority.

The Anabaptist style of biblical interpretation is expressed superbly in a summary statement adopted by the Mennonite Church General Assembly in 1977. The first paragraph of this paper, "Biblical Interpretation in the Life of the Church," states it well:

> The Bible is *the Book of the people of God.* It is the testimony of God's people to the prophetic Word and historic events. Through this Word and these events God created a special people with a peculiar political shape among the nations. Their unique testimony finds understanding and credibility in the ongoing community of faith. The Bible is truly at home within the believing community which gave the Bible its shape. The Bible in turn has shaped the people of God. Thus, it is from the perspective of the faith and life of this community of God's people that the Bible can be interpreted and applied to today's world.

Contrary to Roman Catholicism, biblical interpretation in the Anabaptist tradition does not come from the top. It emerges from the life of the people, from the encounter with other communities of faith, from the necessity of dealing with issues of obedience and common life. Ideally, there is an openness to learn from minority voices and to demonstrate that Scripture is "profitable for reproof and correction" (2 Tim. 4:16). Whenever a biblical truth is neglected by the body, the Spirit inspires certain members to raise up that truth for the edification of all.

In recent years a new Holy Spirit movement has risen to call us to a greater sense of expectancy; at the same time other persons have been used to correct some of the emphases of this same movement. Similarly, dispensationalists have helped us think through our understanding of the kingdom coming. At the same time they have been asked to reexamine some of their assumptions. And again, until very recently most Bible translators have been male. Now women are learning Hebrew and Greek and translating the Bible. The women recognized that Phoebe is called a deaconess (Rom. 16:1), a translation not used in other places when the same word refers to a man. Tradition more than an accurate translation of the text kept Phoebe from being named the minister and leader she really was. All of these examples point to how much we do need one another in our efforts to rightly divide the word of truth.

Contrary to some Protestant tendencies, the Anabaptists did not accept the authority of individual interpretation. In recent trips to Pennsylvania Dutch country, I encountered popular music groups which represent the infiltration of popular Protestant American religion. I found an almost exclusive use of "I language." Contrary to this, our heritage more often uses "we language." Alexander Mack and his group came out of the radical Pietist movement and identified with the older "Baptist" movement of the sixteenth century. One of the major shifts which occurred then was from the "I language" of the separatists to the "we language" of the Bible. Today's pop religion offers prayers to "my God." Biblical language models prayers to "our God." Pop religion proclaims Christ's death for me. Pauline language accents Christ's death for us. Pop religion points almost exclusively to what is a valid theme of accepting Christ as personal Savior. New Testament references, however, name Christ as Savior of Israel and Savior of the world. Those of us who have Pietist roots do not want to give up the focus on the personal and all singular pronouns. If we eliminate all plural pronouns, however, we pervert the very nature of biblical faith.

There may be a few persons who find a Bible on an isolated island or in a hotel room and come to know a fuller truth and a radical change in their life. The Anabaptist perspective, however, asserts that the will of God in Christ as it is revealed in the Bible becomes most apparent to us in relationships in the community. Second Peter 1:20 says it clearly: "First of all you must understand this, that no prophecy of scripture is a matter of one's own interpretation." The next words do suggest that the reason for this is that no prophecy comes by the impulse of men, but by men moved by the Holy Spirit. Some scholars say that this means that the guidance of the Holy Spirit is needed in our

Howard Royer

own interpretation more than it refers to the community interpretation of Scripture. We Anabaptists, however, believe that the Holy Spirit works through and comes to us through the community of faith.

How do we understand and interpret the Bible? Communal consensus can be as tyrannical as the decrees of popes. Historically Catholics have looked to the hierarchy for biblical interpretation. Protestants have relied on biblical scholars and creedal formulations as the key that unlocks the treasures of the Scriptures. The Anabaptist hermeneutic (way of interpreting the Scriptures) has at times seemed to open the door to the worst kind of confusion. For it claims that the entire community is to be relied on for proper understanding. The community, however, does need to choose leaders who will give themselves to the study and teaching of the Bible. The task of such leaders then is not to dictate but rather to persuade. They are to offer insights which are then tested by the community.

This method requires that we take our insights to the community and that our smaller gatherings take their issues to larger gatherings. Telling the story of the Brethren in Christ, Carlton O. Wittlinger writes that they "emphasized corporate rather than private interpretation of Scripture." They followed the precept that "in the multitude of counselors there is safety. When exegetical problems proved too difficult for local districts to solve, such questions normally were passed to General Conference." Such has been the history of each of our groups. Though we are noncreedal people, we must not minimize the importance of the necessary study and work which goes into making our corporate decisions.

At the same time biblical interpretation is the task of each member. In reading about the many martyrs of the faith, one cannot help but be amazed at their saturation in biblical materials. Yet today, even with our abundance of biblical aids, we fall far short in our Bible study. I know one pastor who is teaching his people the biblical languages and then moving from this language study to serious Bible study in the life of the congregation. For most of us, however, the Bible too often remains a strange book. Still awaiting us is a deep and meaningful experience, if we are willing to enter the strange new world of the Bible. For in opening the Book, we can receive the gift.

4.
Law: Freedom From or Freedom For

Scripture Focus: Mark 10:1-16; Galatians; Romans 3.

We seldom had fried preacher at our house for Sunday dinner. My parents were anxious that all five sons have nothing but positive attitudes toward the church and its leadership. Usually we learned about their critical reactions only when they did not know we were listening. Thus it was memorable when, during one Sunday dinner, my mother blurted out: "Bad news, bad news. That's all we have been getting at church lately. How terrible the world is! How difficult it is to live as Christians! I thought the gospel was good news."

Perhaps it was this memory that helped prepare me for an experience I had in seminary. I attended an interseminary conference, a rather large gathering of ministerial students from many different denominations. I bunked in the room of a young Lutheran minister. In our first conversation, he found out where I was from and my denominational identity. "Yes," he replied, "my church history professor was telling us about your people today. He said that you are New Testament Pharisees. Just as the Pharisees derived a strict pattern of laws from Moses, so Christian sects like yours make a law out of the teachings of Jesus."

I was forced to deal with my feelings and questions. Did I agree with what he was saying? How could I defend myself and my people? At that time, I had no quick answer to give. Since that early seminary experience, I have discovered that we are a people who in one way or another are very concerned about the relationship between gospel and law, faith and works, grace and judgment.

Three Uses of the Law

At the time of the Protestant Reformation, the Reformers focused again on what Paul had written about law. Justification by faith rather than justification through works of the law became a central teaching. Out of much discussion there emerged what is called the three uses of the law. These uses have been named half-humorously by some as the law as *prosecutor,* the law as *policeman* (no policewomen then), and the law as *pedagogue* (teacher). It has been jested that from these you can choose your poison. Though these were not the exact labels the Reformers used, they can help us understand some of the issues, both then and today.

For Paul, the law meant the contents of the first five Books of Moses. In a larger sense, the law encompassed the entire Old Testament. Law was also understood as extending beyond written Scriptures to include the oral traditions of the rabbis. All instruction and revelation in both the Scriptures and the oral tradition came together to make up the Torah.

Romans 3:28,31
For we hold that a man is justified by faith apart from works of law. . . . Do we then overthrow the law by this faith? By no means! On the contrary, we uphold the law.

Galatians 5:13-14
For you were called to freedom, brethren; only do not use your freedom as an opportunity for the flesh, but through love be servants of one another. For the whole law is fulfilled in one word, "You shall love your neighbor as yourself."

Paul's major discussion about the law is found in Romans 3 and in Galatians. Paul wrote profoundly on this topic. He packed so much into a few pages. We become aware of the rich variety of literary forms which make up our Bible when we encounter the difficult, brilliant, and profound thought-world of the apostle Paul. He is not always easy to understand. The best we can do is to choose some of his basic themes and attempt to understand them and apply them to our situation.

Law as Prosecutor

Paul asserted that "through the law comes knowledge of sin" (Rom. 3:20). Talking about this text, one of my seminary colleagues relates what has become known as his famous "garbage story." In his family it is his job to take out the garbage. He often is so involved in doing other things, however, that he is not as interested in taking out the garbage as his wife is in having him take it out. He gets irritated if she nags. She may become irritated enough to take out the garbage herself, thereby "heaping coals of fire on his head." In this example it is not the law (the rule that he is to take out the garbage) that is sin. Rather, the law becomes the occasion of sin, namely, the sense of alienation which occurs between husband and wife.

Paul probably wrote his epistle to the Galatians to oppose the influence of the Judaizers among them. The Judaizers were also called the circumcision party because they insisted that in order to be regarded as Christians, Gentiles needed to be circumcised and to observe other aspects of the Jewish law. Paul did not object to the practice of circumcision for Christians who had a Jewish background. He did, however, confront the Judaizers with the question: "How can you compel the Gentiles to live like Jews?" Circumcision was not sin; but in the churches of Galatia the insistence on circumcision became an occasion for the sin of division.

The law might not be such a tough prosecutor if it dealt only with rules like taking out the garbage. But the Lutheran professor was right: For us, the law is also the Sermon on the Mount. That sermon is marvelous. But who among us entirely lives it? This may have been something of what my mother had in mind. Our preachers hold up so many "do's and don'ts," so many high expectations that we become oppressed when we realize how far short we fall in trying to live up to them. If adultery is only the outward act, then we might escape becoming adulterers. In the Sermon on the Mount, however, Jesus may have made each one of us an adulterer, when he talked about the way we look at or think about other persons. Even when we feel we are living up to the teachings of our Lord, we are tempted with self-righteousness, that sin of bad attitudes toward those who fall short of "our" high standards. This brings us to a basic concluding statement of the apostle: "All have sinned and fallen short of the glory of God" (Rom. 3:23).

The consciousness of the law as prosecutor has struck me powerfully in this past decade. I have had to deal with the knowledge of sin which comes with being a male, white, middle-class American. I have become more aware of ways in which I fail to grant sisters equal dignity within the body of the church. I have grown in the knowledge of how my thoughts and actions should be ideally. But life habits, patterns, and privileges crop up again and again.

More painful has been the growing consciousness of how my middle-class lifestyle is a part of a system which is bad news for many of the poor of the world. People who are forced to live on only a few hundred dollars a year and suffer malnutrition from inadequate diets are working in fertile fields which grow coffee or rubber for North Americans. How much better if the land were utilized for their own good.

Hardly a day passes in which I do not think about my involvement in structures which violate other people. I hope I do more than think. I pray, I change some, and I attempt to participate in causes and missions which try to make a difference by witnessing through word and deed. Still I have not been led to forsake my identity, even if such were possible. I am humbled to call on God's grace, and I believe that Jesus loves even me—a white, male, middle-class American.

Martin Luther described the law as an even meaner prosecutor than I have just described. He named the law as God's wrath in action, as God's hammer to beat us down and reduce us to despair. From Luther's commentary on

Galatians we read: "Therefore God must use that hammer, to wit, the Law, to break, beat, pound and, in a word, reduce to nothing that beast with its vain confidence, wisdom, righteousness, and power, that at length it may learn that it is lost and damned." For Luther, this theological use is one of the main functions of the law. It leads us to see how far we fall short of living up to the law. It thereby brings us to our knees before the one who forgives, namely, Jesus, who fulfills the law in all its perfection.

It is right that our heritage has held up the life and teachings of Jesus as the way to be followed. It is also right that we can live in the expectancy that God can grant us power for holy living. However, when we fail to live up to the best we know, we need to learn the good news from the message of Paul and the Reformers.

Law as Policeman

In addition to the law functioning as prosecutor and hammer, the Reformers spoke of the law as necessary for maintaining order in the fallen world. This second function has been named the political use of the law. Here law is not derived from the Sermon on the Mount. Rather rules and regulations evolve out of common-sense applications of worldly wisdom.

Luther believed that fallen humans would completely devour one another without the sword of rulers who serve as a terror to bad conduct (Rom. 13:3). Therefore, the policeman's or soldier's job is to protect the innocent and punish the evil. In personal relationships a person turns the other cheek and lives by the Sermon on the Mount. But a policeman functions as a part of the temporal kingdom which is ordained by God. As an individual, a person lives in the spiritual kingdom. In an office a person serves the temporal laws devised by citizens for the sake of order.

Christians, however, live in both kingdoms at the same time. Luther maintained that a soldier as a Christian could love a person at the same time he was killing the person because the soldier had been officially appointed to protect his neighbors. There is a definite problem with Luther's scheme, however. It divides up our lives into two compartments: As policemen we live by law; as individuals, the gospel forgives and guides our personal lives. Should not the policeman operate by gospel principles as well as by rational principles? Do we not need both law and gospel in our personal relationships?

Such separation of law and gospel is foreign to Paul's teachings. The only place where there seems to be support for this kind of compartmentalization is in Romans 13. The first verse, however, when correctly translated, indicates that God *orders* rather than *ordains* the powers that be. In this way God might work through the policeman for good without necessarily approving actions which are entirely without mercy.

Some expressions of Anabaptism offer an interesting variation on Luther's theme. It is agreed that God ordains policemen and soldiers for the sake of order in our sinful world; but Christians, who live by the gospel, should not be soldiers. Such a view has the advantage of recognizing that we cannot expect the same behavior from unredeemed people as from the redeemed. Its disadvantage, however, lies in appearing not to care whether or not gospel principles become more prevalent in society.

Why is this history so important? Simply because so many people today still think in two-kingdom categories. In church they talk about how people cannot be saved by works of the law but only by grace. In public life, however, they are law-and-order people who advocate stiffer penalties and punishment which far exceeds an "eye for an eye."

I have experienced these views from many persons when I have worked to provide bail money for young men. Rather than wanting to work for reconciliation between the offender and the victim by providing an opportunity for the offender to make things right, many people want to punish the offender in such a way that more money is lost than was stolen in the first place. Similarly, instead of placing offenders in situations in which redemption and restitution might occur, there are strong pressures to put offenders in situations which are, in reality, training schools for crime. This simply creates further alienation from society. In spite of the fact that most offenders are from broken homes and have a great need for love, the general mood in our society desires vengeance and punishment more than forgiveness and redemption.

Granted, society does need protection. More attention needs to be given to the victims of crime. We need laws and justice. But our criminal justice system also needs to be penetrated with large doses of redemption. Both law and gospel are needed.

Law as Pedagogue

The first use of the law (as prosecutor), though painful, may bring us penitently to the gospel. The second use of the law (as policeman) is necessary for the preservation of order, though it can easily degenerate into the practice of vengeance, which belongs only to God (Rom. 12:19). The third use, law as pedagogue (teacher), is more positive. Christians want to do the will of God, and the law helps define what God would have persons do. Paul may sound as if he wants to get rid of the law when he insists that we "are justified by faith apart from works of the law" (Rom. 3:28). Like Jesus, however, Paul never advocates getting rid of the law. "Do we then overthrow the law by this faith? By no means! On the contrary, we uphold the law" (Rom. 3:31).

Luther had what is called a law-gospel scheme. The function of the law, whether of Moses or of Jesus, is to demonstrate that we cannot live the law and thereby bring us to see our need for the gospel of forgiveness. Our response to this forgiveness, then, is grateful thanksgiving. Our faith will become active in love. Luther's ethics come out of a spontaneous response of love for neighbor in appreciation for God's love for us.

Calvin held to a law-gospel-law scheme. He taught the same theological and political uses of the law as did Luther. But Calvin saw the law of Moses returning as a guide for the Christian. The law is a goad to prod us. The Ten Commandments are basic to the ethics of Calvinism. The love of the law which permeated the psalter of David was echoed reverently in the songs sung in Calvin's Geneva.

The Anabaptists may have had a gospel-law-gospel-law scheme, which is to say that they found it difficult to separate the two. This is seen in the concept of filial (family-type) obedience. In a beautiful little writing, *Two Kinds of*

Obedience, coming from the Swiss Brethren between 1525 and 1530, filial obedience is contrasted with servile obedience. Filial obedience has its source in the love of God and responds even though no reward follows. Servile obedience, on the other hand, does as little as possible. Filial obedience comes from inner motivation. Servile obedience comes only in response to commands. The filial person knows the treasure of faith. The servile person's treasures are the works done in order to be pious. "The filial is not contrary to the servile, as it might appear, but is better and higher."

Though this writing may be unfair in identifying servile obedience with the Old Testament and filial obedience almost exclusively with the New Testament, servile obedience may be what Paul had in mind in some of his statements about the law. And it does seem to capture the essence of what Paul had in mind in his desire to hold gospel and law together.

Using the analogy of a parent to a child helps to clarify the meaning of filial obedience. You have known a father who lays down the law to his child. The child obeys only because she is afraid of being punished if she does not obey. If her obedience is based on fear more than on love, she may quickly become disobedient when she leaves her father's house. If she obeys, however, not just because of the rule but also out of a good relationship with her father, she is obeying out of love rather than out of fear. Because she has been loved, she wishes to do what her father wants her to do.

Instead of the filial obedience which resembles Paul's teaching about justification by faith, Anabaptist obedience has too often degenerated into a servile form, a kind of legalism based on making a god of goodness instead of responding to the goodness of God. Too often we have mistranslated Jesus' saying to read, "I am obeying your commandments so that you will love me, Jesus," instead of responding to the one who said, "If you love me, you will keep my commandments" (John 14:15).

Freedom and Law

In conclusion it will be helpful to examine what Paul meant by words like slavery and freedom. In Galatians 5:1 Paul writes of freedom from the yoke of slavery. But Paul's thought runs counter to so many of our ideas of freedom. We think that to be free is to be free from the control of others, from external commands, from restrictions on what we want to do. Paul, however, sees the greatest slavery as being self-centeredness. When we obey the law for selfish reasons, we are still in slavery to sin; we are placing ourselves, rather than God, at the center of existence.

Once we have been set free from self-centeredness, we then "become slaves of righteousness" (Rom. 6:18). This way of reasoning is perplexing for many people. But stay with the apostle, for what he is saying is really pro-

found. Paul maintains that when we become slaves to the will of God, we are following the only way which leads to true freedom—freedom *from* self-centeredness and freedom *for* others. It is like a boy lost in the forest. He is free to go in any direction. His only freedom, however, will come in discovering the right path out and following it. Or think of a ship without a compass lost at sea on a cloudy night. The crew is free to steer in any direction. They will remain lost, however, until they can chart their course by compass, by the stars, or in some other way. Real freedom consists of discovering the way and following it.

Popular concepts of freedom imply that we are free when we can do anything we want. We can be in that situation, however, and still know the worst type of slavery— slavery to our own introverted, selfish existence. At such times we are like the little girl who asked her teacher, "Teacher, do we have to do what we want to do today?" Freedom must mean freedom *from sin* so that there can be freedom *for others.*

This is what Paul meant in Galatians 5:13-14 "For you were called to freedom, brethren; only do not use your freedom as an opportunity for the flesh [meaning life lived out of proper relationships], but through love be servants of one another. For the whole law is fulfilled in one word, 'You shall love your neighbor as yourself.' "

Paul is thinking of this freedom when he responds to a specific situation in the Corinthian church. The women at Corinth were experiencing the freedom of what it meant to be neither male nor female in Christ. They no longer needed to obey the laws which required that they remain silent in the back of the synagogue. In their newfound freedom they were prophesying all at once; some were gossiping and whispering to their husbands. Some persons were outraged about this and tattled to Paul. In his response, Paul admonished them that "God is not a God of confusion but of peace" (1 Cor. 14:33). Paul advised that they should not chatter in church (which some scholars say is the preferred translation instead of speak). They should wait until they get home to ask their questions.

Paul was instructing the Corinthians that their freedom in Christ must be used for the sake of order and peace in the community. This is the same message which some scholars see as central to Paul's beliefs about law and gospel. Paul desired, above all else, to break down the dividing wall of hostility between Jews and Greeks. He sought reconciliation in Christ Jesus between Christians who had been raised by the Jewish law and those who had not. Paul's writings about the relationship between freedom and the law bring to mind Bonhoeffer's "cheap grace" and "costly grace." In that spirit, we can also consider the meaning of cheap and costly freedom.

Cheap freedom is freedom from the commands of others, not freedom from sin, and is centered in self.

Costly freedom is freedom from sin so that there is freedom to be persons for others and for God.

5.
Inner Word
and Outer Word

Scripture Focus: John 5:37-42; 6:63; 16:13; 2 Corinthians 3:6; Ephesians 1:17; 6:17.

We were gathered as friends and members of the Body of Christ for worship in a church basement. The next day a young brother was to go on trial in federal court for violations of the Selective Service law. In this setting the Scripture readings, the words of sisters and brothers, the prayers and the songs took on special meaning, deeply penetrating the soul of each person present. At one point in the service I looked around. Almost everyone was standing, arms linked in a circle of love and support, a powerful symbol of the Spirit's presence through the lives of others. Two young Quakers were on their knees, the palms of their hands touching in prayer; they represented the Spirit's presence speaking through the inner voice of each one, which is then shared with the body. Bibles were visible, and one person was looking intently at her Bible.

Put this all together and you have the Anabaptist hermeneutic, that complicated but shorter expression which describes the way our heritage approaches the Bible. Hermeneutic simply means biblical interpretation with the goal that the ancient text comes alive for us today. The Anabaptist hermeneutic consists of a responding community gathering around the Book so that Christ comes alive. And when this happens, we give the credit to the working of God's Spirit.

The early Anabaptists described this happening by talking about the inner and the outer Word. By the inner Word they meant the unwritten Word or the inner light or voice of God. The outer Word meant the spoken or written Word which meets us from beyond ourselves. This language was very common in sixteenth-century Anabaptism and in the German Pietist movement a century and a half later. After several generations, however, the inner Word came to be associated more with Pietism, while obedience to the outer Word was thought to be most characteristic of Anabaptism.

Since three of our denominations claim both Anabaptist and Pietist rootage and the other two Mennonite bodies admit they have been influenced by later Pietism, it might be helpful to look at the interaction between Anabaptism and Pietism. Vernard Eller views these two streams, Anabaptism and Pietism, as offering a creative tension of checks and balances.

> When the . . . Pietist tendency would slide off into subjectivism . . . and private inspiration . . . it is pulled up short by the demand for concrete, outward obedience to an objective Scriptural norm. Conversely, when the Anabaptist tendency would slide off into formalism, biblical literalism or works-righteousness, it is checked by the reminder that faith is a personal relationship rather than a legal one (Vernard Eller, "On Epitomizing the Brethren," *Brethren Life and Thought*, Vol. 6, Autumn 1966, pp. 50-51).

John 6:63
It is the spirit that gives life, the flesh is of no avail; the words that I have spoken to you are spirit and life.

John 16:13
When the spirit of truth comes, he will guide you into all the truth; for he will not speak on his own authority, but whatever he hears he will speak, and he will declare to you the things that are to come.

In this way, Eller reasons, "Anabaptist influences discipline Pietism as the same Pietist influences inspire Anabaptism." We will examine each side of this tension to see how our ancestors' way of understanding it can be translated for us. With them we want to be faithful to biblical faith. In our study we hope to find guidelines for our use of the Bible itself.

Inner Word

The inner or unwritten Word was variously named the inner light, the inner voice, or inner illumination. The source was God. The location was the heart, the essence of a person's entire being. When we speak of "the heart of a matter," we retain something of the power of the metaphor by referring to our most vital organ. Augustine wrote: "The sound of our word strikes your ears, but the Master is within you." The Quakers derive a similar belief from a favorite text: "The true light that enlightens every man was coming into the world" (John 1:9). The basis for the doctrine of the inner light is this assurance that Christ came and comes to enlighten every person.

Some of the early Anabaptists shared this conviction about the inner Word. Jacob Kautz, formerly a Lutheran, said, "The Word which we speak outwardly with our mouth and write and print is nothing living, nor the eternal Word of God, but only . . . an indication of the inner Word." To make people depend on the outer Word alone, other radicals maintained, makes an idol of the preacher or of Scriptures. The spiritualizers went even further in this direction than the biblically oriented Anabaptists.

The spiritualists minimized or completely denied that God speaks through the church or through Scriptures. They claimed that God speaks directly through dreams or visions. Storch, one of the Zwickau prophets, called Scripture a dead letter, heard voices, denied the validity of all outward baptisms, had visions, wore a long gray robe and broadbrimmed hat, preached that all possessions should be held in common, and advocated taking a new spouse as often as the Spirit led. At Munster other radicals took up the sword to set up an Old Testament theocracy which included, among other things, the practice of polygamy.

The social and religious unrest of that day made it difficult for Luther and other Reformers to differentiate between the various kinds of radicals. In some ways that situation resembled the variety of groups which came together to protest the American military presence in Vietnam: Marxists, Bible-carrying fundamentalists, hippies, Quakers, rebellious adolescents, middle-class church going people, praying charismatics, and liberal activists. The media often lumped them together, creating an impression of wild-eyed radicalism, a single impression I often encountered in our local communities.

From our present perspective it is difficult to be tolerant toward the cruel persecution of the established churches at the time of the Reformation. We can understand, however, the fear of complete chaos which Luther and other Reformers must have experienced. Either too busy or too biased to properly distinguish between the groups, Luther began calling all radicals Schwarmer (enthusiasts) or fanatics. For Luther understood that God came to us and comes to us through the Scriptures, the sacraments, and preaching. He was afraid of what would happen if the outer forms of church, family, and government should lose their authority. In lumping all of his opponents together, Luther charged the Anabaptists with valuing the inner Word at the expense of the written Word. Calvin accused the Anabaptists of confusing "the giddiness of the head with the illumination of the heart."

Obviously, the charges were not fair. Our spiritual ancestors, for the most part, were biblicists. We have seen how they held to a high view of biblical authority and inspiration. They advocated that every Christian should study the Bible. Often the Bible was the only book to be found among their possessions. They knew it thoroughly, amazing both their comrades and their adversaries with their command of the Bible's contents.

The encounter with spiritualism, however, remains with us even today. The current popular fad looks to dreams as a primary source of our knowledge of God and ourselves. I met a brother who shared with me how mistaken the concept of the simple life was. If he did not drive his Cadillac, if he did not wear the finest of clothing, if he did not live in a mansion, he would not be witnessing properly and joyously to how God had blessed him. He was certain he was right because he had been listening to the voice of the Lord. I wondered whether that inner voice represented his own wishes more than the biblical word enlightened by the Spirit of Jesus. All of which makes relevant the advice given in 1 John 4:1-2: "Beloved, do not believe every spirit, but test the spirits to see whether they are of God; for many false prophets have gone out into the world. By this you know the Spirit of God: every spirit which confesses that Jesus Christ has come in the flesh is of God, and every spirit which does not confess Jesus is not of God."

Alexander Mack, one of the first eight who through mutual baptisms began the Church of the Brethren, lived in a time in which people received many kinds of special revelations from God. Many of his neighbors were Inspirationalists, who later became the Amana colonies in Iowa. Prophets emerged among them—prophets whose voices were regarded as being as inspired as the biblical authors' voices. Though he did not reject direct revelations as such, Mack did insist that such revelation be tested by the Scriptures: "This law which is inwardly written by the Spirit of God is completely identical with that which is outwardly written in the New Testament." Mack's focus was somewhat different from the mainline Reformers'. He was open to special forms of revelation such as dreams, but he felt that these must conform to the New Testament. Luther and Calvin would not grant that any such revelation was valid. For them the function of the internal testimony of the Holy Spirit was to convince persons of the truth of what comes through the outer Word.

A vital question for many Christians today is, What kind of attitudes should we have toward other religions? Has God's nature been revealed in ways other than what is found in the Christian story? Alexander Mack would have been open to views which grant the presence of God's truth in other places. He would have said that we discern this presence, however, only through the Way we know in Christ.

This approach supports the witness of missionaries

Bob Taylor

who say that they have discovered in places where Christians had never been before that Christ had already been there. If we were to encounter a group which appeased the gods by sacrificing babies to alligators, we could not name that as God's way. When we encounter a Gandhi, however, who teaches us how to love and deal with enemies, can we not affirm the presence of the Spirit of Christ, the Holy Spirit?

It is not easy for us to agree on how we understand this question. Personally, it is difficult for me to limit the activity of the Holy Spirit to the places and times where Christ has been consciously confessed. However, it is only through the Spirit of Christ as revealed in the Scriptures and in the community that I can discern that which does or does not confess Jesus Christ (see 1 John 4:1-3).

Outer Word

The early Anabaptists were not only accused of giving higher authority to the inner Spirit than to the outer Word. They were also charged with legalism, an adherence to the dead letter of the law rather than to the Spirit which gives life. This may have been to their credit. The fact that they were accused of being both spiritualists and legalists suggests that they probably had a fairly balanced view. Such a balance is seen in some of the early writings.

We have noted that the Anabaptists held that the inner Word needed to be tested by the outer Word. Conversely, many of them testified that the outer Word needed the life-giving Spirit which is necessary for the inner Word to reflect God's Word. It is good to read that the Word became flesh, they taught, but Christ must also become flesh in us. The simple faith of the Swiss Brethren was characterized by a biblical literalism which desired to obey the commands of Christ and his teachings. The word legalism does not apply to them, however, if one means that they only used the New Testament in an external way without regard for its essential spiritual character. They were in agreement with Paul's statement about the new covenant being based on the Spirit more than the written code. "For the written code kills, but the Spirit gives life" (2 Cor. 3:6).

It was difficult for the Anabaptists to understand how

their persecutors could burn and drown them on the basis of biblical authority. This was no doubt the sentiment which evoked the statement that Philip Melanchthon, Luther's close colleague, killed more people with his dead Scripture than all the hangmen. The Pietists felt similarly toward the "dead orthodoxy" which held a high theology about the Bible but disregarded its message of love. The methodology of this orthodox group became known as Protestant scholasticism. It upheld a theory of biblical inerrancy, but ignored ethical or practical applications. The Pietists, however, like the earlier Anabaptists, held to the authority of the Bible and looked to the power of the Holy Spirit, which enabled the sacred writings to become a living force within them.

The same issues remain with us. I will never forget a brother who sharply put down another brother for laying aside his coat before he rose from supper to wash feet: "That's not the way Jesus did it. Jesus rose from supper, then laid aside his garment. We are to do it like Jesus did." As he focused so intently on how and in what order things needed to be done, he seemed to forget the spirit of the feetwashing rite itself. And as I write, I read in the paper about a minister who is concerned that the Word of Scripture come alive. He has rigged a chair with an electric charge so that it shocks children who sit on it. His purpose, he says, is to shock persons into receiving the Word of God. Most of us will judge that this minister is failing to leave enough of this function to the work of the Holy Spirit.

The more our mothers and fathers in the faith dealt with this issue of inner Word and outer Word, the more they came to the conclusion that these are not two Words but one. This must be something of what the writer to the church at Ephesus had in mind: "And take the helmet of salvation, and the sword of the Spirit, which is the word of God" (Eph. 6:17).

Word Coming Alive

In spite of the many attractive aids and literature to help us understand the message of the Bible, the Bible remains a sadly neglected book, even among Christians. We simply have too many other things to look at, to read, and to do. In so many places the Bible is a "dead" book. It is placed on a pedestal or in a corner, or used primarily for the bride to carry down the aisle or as an impressive register in which to record vital family statistics.

But the Spirit refuses to allow the Bible to remain dead. The Spirit gives life and the Bible comes alive again and again for us, in us, and through us. Let's look at some guidelines that will help us read the Bible with a greater degree of openness to the life-giving nature of the Spirit.

1. The Bible needs to be read in the knowledge of what comes before and what follows. Sections need to be interpreted by the Spirit of the entire Bible. A rather crude illustration shows how grossly verses can be taken out of context. A minister leafs through the Bible, quoting three verses successively: "And Judas went out and hanged himself." "Go thou and do likewise." "Whatsoever thou doest, doest quickly."

A better example might be some of the old commandments, such as the one already cited from Leviticus: "For every one who curses his father or his mother shall be put to death" (Lev. 20:9). From this text we can learn something about the basic respect for parents which the Bible expects. In reference to the death penalty, however, the verse needs to be read in light of the mind of Christ and other biblical passages.

2. The historical and cultural background of passages needs to be understood. We need to ask the questions *who, what, where, when, and why.* When we discover the reason for some practice in the early church, then we have the difficult task of deciding whether that practice is still for us today.

This question was highlighted by a New Testament scholar as he talked about the sacraments. He concluded that the word sacrament is not biblical and therefore should not be used. He also dealt with some specifics. He chided those of us who use grape juice for communion. The Bible definitely says wine. The early Christians certainly used wine, not grape juice, he reasoned.

Later in the talk-back session the speaker was questioned about the traditional Pauline passages dealing with covered and uncovered heads. Immediately he replied that only the temple prostitutes appeared without veils. The

Bob Taylor

sisters at Corinth who refused to cover their heads were creating a scandal for the entire community. Since our situation is much different, he reasoned, this symbol is no longer necessary. I promptly reflected on how I had been taught in the same way, but given different conclusions. My mother had explained how unsafe the water was at the time of Jesus. It made sense to use wine then. With better knowledge of the dangers of fermented beverages, grape juice is a better choice today. But in reference to the head covering, my mother felt that Paul's teachings and the practice of the centuries should be followed.

Additional questions may only complicate the difficulty of knowing what was for then and what should be for us today. What about the ex-alcoholics who plead with churches not to use wine in communion as that, in effect, keeps them from communion? And what about women for whom the covering still serves as a powerful symbol of reverence, in much the same way as an uncovered head symbolizes reverence for men? And since people no longer wash feet as a sign of hospitality, would not shining shoes be a more appropriate symbol? On the other hand, many persons protest that there is power in doing something which goes back to Jesus. Woe to me if it appears that I have neat answers. I simply want to suggest that we need to struggle together to translate ancient faith and practices for our own day and times.

Anna Mow tells about a Hindu priest who meditated so long in one posture that he was bothered by rats nibbling away at his body. So he tied a cat nearby. Centuries passed. Meditation at that spot became incorporated into a temple. Cats, and all kinds of rules and regulations about them, continued as a part of the meditation atmosphere. Few people, however, knew why the cats were there.

Anna was describing what is known as a broken symbol, one which has lost its meaning and consequently its power. We must be careful lest our symbols become broken. When they do, it does not necessarily mean that they must be eliminated. It does mean that we should study anew why the symbol emerged in the first place, study what its meaning was then and through the years, and determine if a meaningful revival of its message is possible for our time.

3. We need to consider how the text has been inter-preted by others. We need the guidance of those who know the biblical languages and have spent a great deal of time in study. We can be helped by knowing how Christians in other periods in history and in other traditions have inter-preted a text.

One interesting study is to look at how New Testament writers used the Old Testament. From what books did they most often quote? What themes did they choose to talk about the significance of the life and death of our Lord? We need to use various translations and give more credence to versions made by a committee than to translations and paraphrases prepared by individuals such as Moffatt, Phillips, Good News for Modern Man, and The Living Bible.

The Living Word

When I was a pastor and spent more time knocking on doors, I occasionally discovered persons who were bitterly disillusioned with the Bible. In listening to their stories, I often found that they had been deceived, rejected, or mistreated by a minister, parent, or teacher who claimed to believe in the Bible from Genesis to Revelation. These disillusioned persons associated the Bible with the bad taste left by persons who appeared to be so hypocritical. In such cases a lot of loving patience is needed to help per-sons change from identifying the Bible with deception to identifying the Book with trusting, loving honest people.

And yet such change is possible. And such change is needed if the outer Word is to be received as the living Word, the one Word of truth and life.

6.
The Life-Giving Spirit With Us

Scripture Focus: Genesis 1:2; Exodus 31:3; Psalm 51:10; Isaiah 11:2; Joel 2:28; Mark 1:10; Luke 11:13; John 16:13ff.; Acts 2:1ff.; 1 Corinthians 3:16-17.

Caricatures are usually exaggerations which, nevertheless, contain a grain of truth. Such may be the case with the description a Radical Pietist immigrant in 1750 gave of four churches on one intersection in a certain beautiful city (Philadelphia). For our purposes we will omit the Quakers and the Ephrata community in order to focus on the satiric wit in these sketches of the Mennonites and Brethren (Dunkers). The first description is obviously of the Mennonites.

> The house . . . seemed to be rather old as it was patched in many places. Above the door had been placed two men. One of them was blindfolded, and the sighted one led him by the staff. Above this was written: "Because we lack the power of the word, we content ourselves with the dead letter." These . . . are upright in their conduct. They wear plain clothing. Most of the men wear beards. When they are grown they are baptized. A little water is poured over their heads. Their meetings are often very sleepy affairs.

Though the author reported that the Dunker house struck the eye because of its beautiful color, a Dunker meeting does not fare any better under the scrutiny of his pen.

> Over the door was a lamp which had been knocked over with this inscription above it: "We sing and preach with great outcry, if only the spirit could be thereby." . . . Their clothing is middle-class. Most of the men wear beards. They do not tolerate infant baptism. When they become adults and wish to be baptized, they go where water is and have themselves immersed three times. They hold communions or love feasts often. Their meetings are zealous and their preaching and praying often take place with great clamor, as if their God could not hear them well. One hymn chases another as if they lack [inner] silence. They teach their cherished truths after the letter (Donald F. Durnbaugh, "Relationships of the Brethren with the Mennonites and Quakers, 1708-1865," *Church History,* Vol. 35, March 1966, p. 42).

The writer implies a Spirit deficiency in both groups. The Mennonites lack it. The Brethren (Dunkers) attempt to compensate for their deficiency by making a lot of noise. Are these caricatures fair, either then or today? What and who is the Holy Spirit? How do we know the presence of the Spirit?

Genesis 1:1-2

In the beginning God created the heavens and the earth. . . . and the Spirit of God was moving over the face of the waters.

1 Corinthians 3:16-17

Do you not know that you are God's temple and that God's Spirit dwells in you? If any one destroys God's temple, God will destroy him. For God's temple is holy, and that temple you are.

The Life-Giving Spirit

"In the beginning God created the heavens and the earth. The earth was without form and void, and darkness was upon the face of the deep; and the Spirit of God was moving over the face of the waters" (Gen. 1:1-2). Our first reference to the Spirit is found in the second verse of the Bible. The story of creation begins with the affirmation that God created and then tells us how the wind or Spirit of God was moving over the formlessness and void of the earth. The Hebrew word for Spirit, *ruach,* literally means breath or wind. Through God's breathing, chaos becomes cosmos (an orderly universe).

Ruach can also mean a windstorm or mighty wind. This figure of speech, along with "tongues of fire," was later used to describe another beginning, the birth of the church at Pentecost (Acts 2). Wind, fire, power, and life are all words close in meaning to the word Spirit. When we ask whether a school or a team has spirit, we are basically inquiring whether there is really life and vitality. The Holy Spirit alludes to God's activity in giving life. The creation story is also our story. Life began with each of us as God's gift, when God breathed into our nostrils (Gen. 2:7).

Genesis 1:2 could also read, "The Spirit of God was swooshing or hovering over the . . . waters," perhaps beating its wings. In Deuteronomy 33:11 we have the same Hebrew word used to describe an eagle hovering over her little ones, beating her wings in order to coach them to fly. In later rabbinic tradition the bird of Genesis 1:2 was said to be a dove. This reminds us of Jesus' baptism: "He saw the heavens opened and the Spirit descending upon him like a dove" (Mark 1:10). And in yet another story relating to a lot of water, Noah sent out a dove as a sign of a new creation, a new age. This may help explain why the Hebrew word for Spirit, *ruach,* is generally feminine. In many places, if we were literally faithful to the biblical text, the third person of the trinity would be translated as she or her.

When I was a boy, our trip home from Sunday night church services took us through the black community. When the windows of the black church were up, we rolled our car windows down to enjoy the spirit and power of the singing. But I remember how patronizing we sometimes were. "If they would become intelligent and sophisticated like us," we thought, "then their worship would be more civilized like ours." Recently, through preaching experiences in the black community, I have been amazed at the spirit of participation and support which is present. As a result I have shared with blacks that though I do not understand much about "soul," I know that whatever it is, they must keep it. And I wish we had more of it in the faith communities in which I worship.

Often people complain that a congregation or a church service is cold. When such a statement is shared, it is often difficult to know exactly what is meant. For the

Bob Taylor

most part, the person is expressing a hunger for greater warmth in relationships, more "soul" in worship, and perhaps a desire for genuine commitment to Christ and the church. Some of us are grateful to the charismatics for influencing us to be freer in terms of loving God with our hearts and emotions as well as our minds. It is often awkward for many in my generation to visibly demonstrate emotions or affection. We wonder whom and when to embrace. We are often embarrassed. But it is good to experience some genuine signs so that others may really "know we are Christians by our love." In our larger cultural setting we know that many people find security in horrible bombs, glorify violence, and worship at the altar of death. Both in our congregation and in the wider culture of which we are a part, we need to feature the message that "the Spirit gives life" (2 Cor. 3:6).

The obvious danger in all of this is that we might equate emotionalism with Spirit. Nazi Germany knew a tremendous outburst of enthusiasm and zealous support for the racist and militaristic policies of the Führer. Such fanatical zeal, however, is not to be equated with the Holy Spirit. Mennonite Brethren learned that coldness in the life of a congregation may lead to a hyperemotional movement which includes dancing, leaping, and shouting. Though this awakening among the Russian Mennonites produced much fruit, historians now recognize the dangers of excessive emotionalism. "These brethren lacked the spirit of discernment and could not differentiate between true Christian joy, which is the fruit of the Spirit, and an emotional ecstasy which is psychological or sensual in nature" (J. A. Toews, *A History of the Mennonite Brethren Church,* p. 60). Similarly, some charismatics in their valid concern about the "deadness" of much contemporary Christianity have over-reacted and have minimized the part of the commandment which asks us to "love God with all our minds."

It is not enough to get excited. What is crucial is what we are excited about. In our success-oriented culture, we are tempted to feel that any movement which is prospering, growing, and influential must have the Lord's blessing. But whatever has spirit does not necessarily have the Holy Spirit, the Spirit of our Lord. The psalmist teaches us to pray, "Create in me a clean heart, O God, and put a new and steadfast spirit within me" (Psa. 51:10). We are to rejoice in the new; but we are also to seek a steadfast spirit, one which will remain faithful when there is not much excitement, when things are not all going our way, and when we are taking orders from a different drummer than that of most of our contemporaries.

Another danger with the focus on powerful manifestations of the Spirit is that we may be tempted to want to capture and program the Spirit. We can learn from the brother who had his conversion experience when he fell into a well. He then proceeded to push others into wells so that they might have a great experience like his. In our enthusiasm we are tempted to plan for the Spirit's power and presence to encounter others exactly as it encountered us.

One prayer group prayed fervently for the miraculous recovery of a sister. They learned that she did take a sudden turn for the better. But their concern was more to find out whether her recovery occurred when they were praying than it was to praise God for her healing. We need to live with expectancy and yet, at the same time, we need to recognize that the Spirit, like the wind, "blows where it will." God's Spirit moves with freedom. The Spirit cannot be caught or possessed. Rather, one must be possessed and moved by the Spirit (John 3:8).

The Spirit With Us

"Do you not know that you are God's temple and that God's Spirit dwells in you? If any one destroys God's temple, God will destroy him. For God's temple is holy, and that temple you are" (1 Cor. 3:16-17). For a long time this has been a great temperance text for me. Since my body is God's temple in which the Spirit dwells, it is to be treated with reverence through good nutrition, personal habits, exercise, and sleep. I still like this theology, though it may not have been what Paul really had in mind.

Paul was writing to warn those who were intentionally destroying the life of the community. To fail to show deep concern for the good of the body (the community) is the same as desecrating a temple. As pagans believed that gods lived in their temples, Christians believe that the community is the real temple in which the Spirit of God is found.

Our denominations will not agree on all of the topics related to the doctrine of the Holy Spirit. On this issue of the Spirit of God being in the community, however, we are close to consensus. For this may be the unique free church contribution to the doctrine of the Spirit. Our heritage has felt strongly the truth of Paul's teaching that the Holy Spirit comes to us through the life of the community. The Anabaptist teaching has been that we cannot relate to God apart from relationships with brothers and sisters. Our rites and ordinances assume that we cannot long separate the two

greatest commandments. How can any one love God, who cannot be seen, unless there is also the love of the neighbor who can be seen (1 John 4:20)?

Peter Riedemann in his *Confession of Faith* interprets the presence of Christ in communion in a way that is unique in Christendom. Christians have heatedly debated whether the bread actually becomes the physical body of Christ or whether there is some kind of bodily or spiritual presence of Christ in the bread. Our heritage, however, has accented Christ's presence with the body, the people, as they break bread together.

Graydon Snyder, a colleague and teacher of New Testament, has carefully examined the text which is usually translated, "This is my body." He claims that a more accurate translation would be, "You are my body." Bread as a part of the goodness of God's creation can be sacred; nevertheless, the primary locus of the real presence of Christ is in the body (the community). A favorite painting, "The Presence," hangs on the wall in my office. Quaker sisters with fully covered heads and Quaker brothers wearing broadbrimmed hats sit in the meeting. And in the midst of the meeting is seen the silhouetted figure of Christ. The gathering is the temple of the Holy Spirit. Christ's presence in the meeting means that he is the teacher. The people gathered constitute his resurrected body.

The laying on of hands is a beautiful biblical symbol which points to the truth that the Holy Spirit comes to us through the community of faith. Thus the letter to Timothy: "Hence I remind you to rekindle the gift of God that is within you through the laying on of my hands" (2 Tim. 1:6).

This provides a possible explanation for some puzzling New Testament passages. The book of Acts relates Paul's conversion experience. Three times the story is told of Paul's encounter with the risen Christ on the Damascus road. Certainly the Spirit was present. One account says, however, that it was not until the end of the journey, when Paul met Ananias and hands were laid on him, that his sight was restored and he was filled with the Holy Spirit (Acts 9). A similar experience concerns those who had been baptized by Philip in Samaria. They had been baptized in the name of Jesus. But not until they sent for Peter and John and hands were laid on them did they receive the Holy Spirit (Acts 8:14-17).

Are these stories reporting some magiclike electric charge transmitted by the laying on of hands? No. One story itself denies this (Acts 8:18-24). These stories are pointing to the truth that the receiving of the Holy Spirit is intertwined in our relationships with the church. Carlton O. Wittlinger puts it well in defining the meaning of conversion in the life of the Brethren in Christ: "To be converted or born again, therefore, was not only to have a subjective salvation experience; it was also to accept the brotherhood understanding of the Christian life" (*Quest For Piety and Obedience,* p. 41).

A student transferred from a Quaker school to ours. After several months he explained one difference he had found between the Quakers and the Brethren. "The Quakers come together in order to share their experiences with the Lord. You Church of the Brethren people seem to come together in order to have an experience."

Though this chapter has focused strongly on the Spirit's activity in the corporate body, we must recognize that our heritage has also stressed the need for the personal presence of the Spirit in the life of the individual believer. The following sermon offers some reflections on the Spirit's presence both in the community and in the individual Christian's life.

Sermon: You Have the Holy Spirit

Text: "If you then, who are evil, know how to give good gifts to your children, how much more will the heavenly Father give the Holy Spirit to those who ask him?" (Luke 11:13). Theme Song: Blessed Assurance, the Spirit Is Mine.

As I grew up in church, the songs and the reading of Scriptures seemed to be full of references to the Holy Ghost. This seemed somewhat spooky, even scary at times. It did convey a spirit of mystery and of reverence. This was good, for we never want to forget that God is always too great for any of us to completely get our arms around. God always remains beyond our little systems. God remains free from our ability to manipulate.

If God remains too mysterious, however, we lose any sense that God is with us. Many persons listen to how

Paul M. Schrock

powerfully the Spirit has worked in the lives of others. They wonder why it has not happened in the same way to them. They need the assurance that God does give the Holy Spirit to those who ask. For this reason it may be helpful to read this sermon of assurance in a way which agrees, "Yes, this has been a part of my experience!" or asks, "Can I know and feel this kind of presence more?"

You have seen a mother nursing or caring for her child in a way which models one who is truly a person for others. Have you ever seen in this picture something of the Spirit of our Lord? Have you received from your mother or another person the love which has been given because she is a part of the community of faith which goes back to Jesus? If you have, *you have received the Holy Spirit.*

Has any one placed hands on you to encourage you, to comfort you, to admonish you in the Spirit of Jesus? If so, *accept the reality that you have received the Spirit.*

Have you ever awakened in the middle of the night and suddenly received an answer to a matter with which you had been struggling for weeks? Though the answer may need to be tested by Scripture and with others, *you may have heard the voice of the Spirit.*

Has the church ever laid hands on you to commission you for a task, to call you for a special ministry, to anoint you for healing? If so, *you received the Holy Spirit.*

Have you ever memorized or known Scriptures and then suddenly had a passage come alive as never before with new freshness and meaning? If so, *the Holy Spirit was bringing life.*

Did you ever face a crisis, not knowing what you might say or what you would do, and then find that you were given the right words to say and the right course of action to take? If so, *you experienced something of the power of the Holy Spirit.*

Did you ever feel depressed about yourself and your situation and then be led through it all so that you could affirm, "I am somebody. God has a purpose for even me." If so, *you received the power of the Spirit to bring newness.*

If you, then, who are evil, know how to give good gifts to others, *how much more will God give the Holy Spirit to you.*

80

The Presence of the Spirit

I have tested this sermon orally at a Keystone Bible Institute in a class with many Mennonites and a sprinkling of Brethren and Brethren in Christ. Likewise, I have received, from helpful critics, some honest feedback about my efforts to put the sermon into writing. Generally, brothers and sisters have approved the intent of my illustrations. They respond that it is right to illustrate that not everyone's experience of the Spirit is the same. Some of us, when intimidated by the spiritually elite, need assurance that we too have received the Spirit. We must not define too narrowly the time, the place, and the nature of the Holy Spirit's work.

But hearers and readers have also expressed basic reservations about this sermon. By labeling such a broad diversity of experiences as the Spirit's work, the specific work of the Spirit in every believer can be minimized. By universalizing the work of the Spirit to include all manifestations of the Spirit of Jesus, confusion instead of clarity may be the end result. It may be right to defend persons who are depressed or threatened when they hear glowing testimonies of experiences which they have never had. At other times, however, it is appropriate that such testimonies lead us to reflect on our spiritual inadequacies. We may be threatened because we are concerned about what might happen if the Spirit really would come with power in our lives.

I may continue to preach this little sermon. We need the assurance of the presence of the Spirit wherever we discern the Spirit of our Lord. But we also need to seek with greater zeal the biblical gifts of the Spirit: the gifts of conviction, repentance, saving faith, deliverance from sin, and empowerment for witness and service.

7.
Filled With the Spirit

Scripture Focus: Luke 1:15, 41; Acts 2:1-4; 4:8, 31; 7:55; 11:24; 13:9, 52; Ephesians 1:23; 3:19; 5:18-20.

In the story of creation we come alive as God breathes into our nostrils the breath of life (Gen. 2:7). The biblical word for breath literally means wind or spirit. The in-breathing or inspiration of God is both the Spirit and the work of the Spirit. Biblical faith regards life as a gift, to which the only proper response is thanksgiving. The quality of life or Spirit which God intended in creation is restored when we embody something of the Spirit which was in Jesus. Then we can point to the presence of the Holy Spirit.

We may be assured of the presence of the Spirit but be puzzled by talk about being filled with the Spirit. Many questions emerge about phrases such as "Holy Spirit baptism," "entire sanctification," "full Gospel," and "the Pentecostal experience." In response to expressions like these, some people get excited, others become confused, and still others are turned off or angered by those who are excited.

Any claim of "being filled with the Spirit" brings out a fulness of emotions and a variety of perspectives. It is virtually impossible to reach a consensus on this issue for one denomination, let alone for five. Nevertheless, this chapter will consider what the Scriptures, our heritage, and our present church life say about being filled with the Spirit. I write as one who has been deeply influenced by contemporary manifestations of the Spirit movement and also as one who is regarded as a friendly critic.

In reflecting on this issue, there will be occasional references to electricity. As in the case of most analogies, this one may make some connections; it may also, at times, short-circuit what would be most helpful. And, as you are already thinking, it may blow some fuses. The choice of electricity as an analogy has several advantages. We depend upon it so much; yet we do not know much about it. We cannot see it, though we see much of what it does. And so it is with the Spirit.

Birth of the Church

On the day of Pentecost, the wind filled all the house, and all were filled with the Holy Spirit (Acts 2:1-4). From that day to the present, Pentecost has been the time to celebrate the birth of the church. The doctrine of the church and the doctrine of the Holy Spirit are intimately related in the dogma and in the celebrations of Christians.

The feast of Pentecost or unleavened bread was an occasion to celebrate a great communal experience with God. Among other things, it pointed back to the appearance of God in wind and fire on Mount Sinai (Exod. 19—20). As there were twelve tribes gathered at the foot of that mountain, so too were there twelve apostles meeting in a house in Jerusalem. A tradition had developed among the rabbis that God's voice had gone out in seventy tongues to offer the Ten Commandments to the neighboring peoples. Only after they refused, did God speak to Israel. In his Pentecost story, Luke may have been consciously recording a wonderful reversal. For here God's presence comes powerfully to those who proclaim the gospel in other tongues, and this gospel was heard by many people in their own languages. And the people responded enthusiastically.

In the prologues to both his gospel and his history, Luke shows the relationship between the missionary beginning of the church and the birth of Jesus. This relationship between God's manifestation at Pentecost and the announcements of the angels in the birth narratives seems to be intentional. Luke brings these two events together with the identical phrase "filled by the Spirit." It is found in both prologues. Throughout the other chapters of his gospel only Jesus is described as "full of the Spirit." Before Pentecost, Luke speaks of the Holy Spirit as something which will only come later with power (Acts 1:8).

In the birth stories and after Pentecost, however, Luke records that persons are "filled with the Holy Spirit." The small circle around Mary experienced Pentecost. John (Luke 1:15), Elizabeth (1:41), and Zechariah (1:67) are reported to have been "filled with the Holy Spirit." John leaps for joy in Elizabeth's womb as Elizabeth, filled with the Holy Spirit, exclaims with a loud cry to Mary: "Blessed are you among women" (1:41-45). Luke seems to be indicating that this small group around Mary was a community of praise and prophecy similar to the type of community that the church, beginning with Pentecost, was to become.

This communal understanding of what it means to be filled with the Spirit can also be found elsewhere in the New Testament. Whenever the Greek word *pleroma* is used for fulness, it is used in a corporate rather than in an individualistic sense. The word is attributed to Christ in Colossians 2:9 and is followed by this affirmation: "and you [plural] have come to fulness of life in him." Likewise in Ephesians 1:23, it is the church that is named the fulness of Christ's body. Similarly the desire that the Ephesians "be filled with all the fulness of God" is found in a passage addressed to them and to all the saints (Eph. 3:14-19).

Genesis 2:7
Then the LORD God formed man of dust from the ground, and breathed into his nostrils the breath of life; and man became a living being.

Acts 2:2-4
And suddenly a sound came from heaven like the rush of a mighty wind, and it filled all the house where they were sitting. And there appeared to them tongues as of fire, distributed and resting on each one of them. And they were all filled with the Holy Spirit and began to speak in other tongues, as the Spirit gave them utterance.

Now for the analogy. We might say that fulness means that all parts of an electric motor are functioning properly, rather than only one part or a few parts receiving more juice than the others. Thus fulness, being filled with the Spirit, is a communal experience.

Power for Bold Personal Witness

The phrase "filled with the Spirit" can also mean a momentary experience which grants power and courage to an individual in a particular situation. The analogy here would be the extra surge of power which allows a machine to operate briefly with high efficiency. The apostle Peter needed such additional power after he healed the blind man. Peter found himself on the spot before the Sanhedrin. The tense of the verb "to fill" which is used in this text suggests that the Spirit enabled Peter at that particular time to witness at great risk (Acts 4:8). After Peter was released with John, the account of a fervent prayer meeting indicates that "they were all filled with the Holy Spirit and spoke the word of God with boldness" (v. 31). Again this momentary surge of power is indicated when the same phrase is used in Paul's dramatic rebuke of Elymas, the sorcerer (13:9). Similarly, Luke described Stephen as being filled by the Holy Spirit at the moment of his martyrdom (7:55-56).

Quality of Character

At times in Scripture, the adjective rather than the verb form of the word is used; instead of "to be filled," we find "to be full of the Spirit." This is applied to our Lord following his baptism: "And Jesus, full of the Holy Spirit, returned from the Jordan" (Luke 4:1). In the selection of the seven deacons, the apostles requested that the church "pick out from among you seven men of good repute, full of the Spirit and of wisdom" (Acts 6:3). In describing the commissioning of Barnabas for leadership in the church at Antioch, Luke reported that he "was a good man, full of the Holy Spirit and of faith" (11:24). In these passages, to be "full of the Holy Spirit" does not refer to a momentary gift for a specific witness but to a more permanent life of grace. "Full" signifies someone who is habitually governed by the Spirit as was Jesus. In terms of our analogy, we know that the motor is sound and good because it is constantly in tune with its source of power.

Second Work of Grace: Entire Sanctification

The above focus on the quality of character provides the biblical basis for what was to develop in Wesleyan revivalism. John Wesley emphasized the importance of a conversion experience which included both *justification,* God's acceptance of the sinner, and *regeneration,* a real change or new birth. The converted person, Wesley emphasized, should grow in grace.

Some persons in the Methodist movement began to testify to the experience of full sanctification, which has come to be known as entire sanctification, as the second

Holy Spirit, Come

1. *Holy Spirit, come with power*
   Breathe into our aching night.
   We expect you this glad hour
   Waiting for your strength and light.
   We are fearful, we are ailing,
   We are weak and selfish too;
   Break upon your congregation,
   Give us vigor, life anew.

2. *Holy Spirit, come with fire*
   Burn us with your presence new.
   Let us as one mighty choir
   Sing our hymn of praise to you.
   Burn away our wasted sadness
   And enflame us with your love;
   Burst upon your congregation
   Give us gladness from above.

3. *Holy Spirit, bring your message,*
   Burn and breathe each word anew.
   Deep into our tired living
   Till we strive your work to do.
   Teach us love and trusting kindness
   Bare our arms to those who hurt;
   Breathe upon our congregation
   And inspire us with your Word.

May be sung to the tune of: "All the Way My Savior Leads Me," "Glorious Things of Thee Are Spoken," "Joyful, Joyful, We Adore Thee," and "Come, Thou Fount."

Words to the hymn "Holy Spirit, Come" copyright 1983 by Anne N. Rupp.

work of grace, "praying through," the second blessing, or Christian perfection. The Holiness movement has also referred to this experience as the infilling or baptism of the Holy Spirit. Though John Wesley never testified to this experience for himself and though he stressed the possibility of losing it (backsliding), he did accept the authenticity of many who claimed the power of this "second work of grace" in their lives. He developed a doctrine of Christian perfection which he defined primarily as perfect love. Wesley held to a dynamic view of a gradual work of sanctification both before and after the possibility of a second definite instantaneous experience.

In the last half of the nineteenth century, a revival of this doctrine appeared in Methodist circles. It grew into what is named the Holiness movement. The Brethren in Christ came in touch with the camp meeting quest for the experience of full sanctification. Out of their Pietist heritage of a heartfelt conversion experience and their history of desiring perfect obedience in their daily walk, many Brethren in Christ were naturally attracted to the Holiness movement. Their preference for "grace of cleansing completed" to "second definite work of grace" in their 1910 conference statement indicates that their position may have been close to the tension which the Wesley brothers felt. John Wesley once pressed his brother Charles to stress the instantaneous work so as to leave him more time for the gradual work, which he felt to be more his calling. Both of the Wesley brothers have had spiritual descendants among the Brethren in Christ.

A similar difference had existed earlier between the two most influential leaders of German Pietism. Both Philip J. Spener and August H. Francke focused on the need for regeneration, a born-again experience for Christians. However, Spener, whose own spiritual growth developed without sudden struggles, storms, or changes, believed that the ways of God are different with each person. With some, conversion will be gradual; with others, it will be sudden. Though in later years Francke allowed the same latitude, the great change and penitential struggle which accompanied his own conversion experience provided the model for later Pietist revivalism.

It has been the same with the second experience. Whether we believe in a more gradual or a very definite work of sanctification, the Holiness movement relates the presence of the Holy Spirit with the quality and character of the life of the believer. The Wesleyan emphasis upon "purity of heart" and "holiness of life" has a definite kinship with the discipleship concerns of Anabaptism. It is not surprising, therefore, that Anabaptist-related groups, such as the Brethren in Christ, have been open to holiness manifestations.

Second Work of Grace: The Pentecostal Experience

Toward the end of the nineteenth century some persons in the Holiness movement began to advocate a third experience. This was the baptism of the Holy Spirit with its resulting manifestations of the gifts of the Spirit, especially the gift of tongues. Some Pentecostal groups, such as the Church of God Prophecy, retain this possibility of three distinct experiences. For the most part, however, the Holiness and Pentecostal movements have developed as distinct families in the twentieth century. As Spirit movements with a common heritage, they often feel a great amount of tension over the nature of the second experience.

Pentecostals, for the most part, replaced the experience of second-work holiness with a focus on Spirit baptism which was associated with the receiving of gifts. They proclaimed the possibility of Pentecostal power and miraculous gifts for us today. Pentecostalism within most denominations is known as the neo-Pentecostal or the charismatic movement. Its members sometimes speak of being "born again" in such a way that others are uncertain whether they are referring to the first conversion experience or to Holy Spirit baptism.

Pentecostals see the New Testament as describing two baptisms for the believer. The first experience is water baptism and is for conversion. Holy Spirit baptism is a definite second experience. One text that supports their understanding is Matthew 3:11, where John the Baptist states, "I baptize you with water for repentance, but he who is coming after me is mightier than I . . . he will baptize you with the Holy Spirit and with fire." A second text is likewise cited to support a two-stage passage into full faith.

Paul M. Schrock

Bob Taylor

In Acts 8, we find Samaritan believers who were baptized in the name of Jesus but who did not receive the Spirit immediately. They received the Spirit only when Peter and John, having arrived from Jerusalem, laid hands on the believers. The same passage has been used by Roman Catholics to point to the need for confirmation in addition to baptism.

Among the most favorite passages cited to support a two-stage baptism is the story of the twelve whom Paul met at Ephesus. Paul asked if they had received the Holy Spirit when they believed. They responded, "We have never even heard that there is a Holy Spirit." When it was revealed that they had been baptized only into John's baptism, they were baptized again in the name of the Lord Jesus. "And when Paul had laid his hands upon them, the Holy Spirit came on them; and they spoke with tongues and prophesied" (Acts 19:1-7). The Pentecostal denominations, as well as the so-called neo-Pentecostals within other denominations, believe that these examples are biblical evidence of the need for two baptisms.

Scholars outside of this circle conclude that Luke is

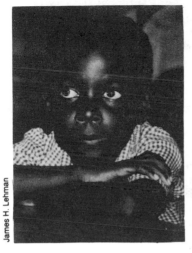

not that interested in providing a scheme of Christian initlation. In the narratives about the early Christians, the receiving of the Spirit at times follows baptism (Acts 2:39ff.) and at other times it comes before baptism (10:44-48). And sometimes those who have been baptized demonstrate an almost complete lack of the Spirit (8:13, 21-22). Concerning the twelve at Ephesus (19), these scholars see the importance of examining the context of the passage. Many persons who were influenced by the early Christians had been previously baptized by John for repentance, forgiveness of sins, and participation in the community of those who lived in expectation of the coming kingdom. This passage does not indicate that they were already Christians. As in the case of others who had been baptized by John, what is named Spirit baptism involves their becoming Christians for the first time.

Six of the New Testament references to two baptisms point to the difference between John's baptism and the baptism Jesus would bring. After Pentecost there was generally no longer a need for a second baptism. This may have been the difference beween the 120 gathered in the house and the 3000 on the day of Pentecost. The 120 may have received John's baptism, but they had not yet realized the full reality of the presence and power of the Spirit of the resurrected Christ. After powerful manifestations of the Spirit, however, Peter could preach to the multitudes, "Repent, and be baptized every one of you . . . for the forgiveness of sins and you shall receive the gift of the Holy Spirit" (Acts 2:38). The blessings of water baptism and Spirit baptism were theirs at once. Cornelius discovered the same when Peter declared: "Can any one forbid water for baptizing these people who have received the Holy Spirit just as we have?" (10:47).

However we come out in reference to the biblical evidence, the Spirit should lead us to a tolerance of both those who testify to a beautiful second baptism as well as those who witness to the continual gradual work of the Spirit coming from their initial or renewed commitment to the Lord.

Expecting Too Little or Thinking More Highly

As is often the case, the differing sides on this issue have something to learn from each other. Pentecostals can teach us that we should live with great expectancy about what the Spirit can do with us and through us. It is a psychological as well as a spiritual truth that when we do not expect much, not much will happen. Michael Green in his book *I Believe in the Holy Spirit* describes many of us too well (p. 146):

> They have been satisfied with a low level of spirituality. They have not allowed God to release them in prayer and praise and personal relationships, from the imprisonment of age-long inhibitions. They have not expected to see God at work in conversions, in changing tough lives, in healing, in explicit guidance. They have forgotten that the manifestations of the Spirit in the New Testament had an uncomfortably concrete nature. Much of the division in the churches that has come with the Pentecostals, has not been the fault of the Pentecostals themselves, but the narrow, fearful,

unspiritual Christianity in whose lukewarm waters many of us have for so long been willing to stay, terrified to launch out into the deep of experience of God.

On the other hand, a pitfall or danger in the Spirit movement may be the possibility of thinking of oneself "more highly than one ought to think." If a person knows Holy Spirit baptism, there may be the temptation to lack charity toward those who seem to be closed to such an experience. Sometimes the person who speaks the most about being full of the Spirit seems to be governed by other spirits, such as arrogance, divisiveness, and lack of love. This certainly is not true, however, of many who regard themselves as Pentecostals or neo-Pentecostals.

Similarly the joyous response of the person who has experienced the gift of healing may convey to others that they too could be healed if they had the same kind of faith. But saints who have lived faithfully and still are ill may hear the healed brother or sister saying, "I have great faith, but you do not." Likewise, those baptized by the Holy Spirit may be so caught up in exercising wonderful gifts that they ignore the call to take up the cross, which might mean suffering as the result of nonconformity to the fallen world.

Possessed by the Spirit
A further look at Ephesians 5:18-20 will conclude our consideration of this difficult yet fascinating topic of being Spirit-filled: "And do not get drunk with wine, for that is debauchery; but be filled with the Spirit." John Stott, in his booklet *The Baptism and Fullness of the Holy Spirit,* offers three helpful concluding statements concerning these verses.

First, the verb "be filled" is plural in this text. This means that the fulness of the Spirit is not a privilege reserved for only a few. Second, the verb is in the present tense. Since the present tense in Greek describes continuing action, the translation might well read, "Keep on being filled with the Spirit." This does not rule out dramatic or decisive experiences; it does mean that we are always open to the continual activity of the Spirit. Third, the verb "be filled" is in the passive voice. We cannot manipulate the Holy Spirit as much as we can relate to and yield to the Spirit. In terms of our electricity analogy, we need to recognize that we may attempt to plug in or plug out the Spirit. But we must never forget that the source of power does not come from ourselves; it comes from beyond.

The word "filled" can be translated "possessed." The Spirit-possessed life is illustrated by a story told about Dwight L. Moody. He was invited to be the guest preacher for an evangelistic crusade. When the local ministers met for planning, one of them expressed reservations about this type of effort. He asked, "Why must it be D. L. Moody? Does he have a monopoly on the Holy Spirit?" "No," replied one of his colleagues, "the Holy Spirit has a monopoly on D. L. Moody."

8.
Identifying the Gifts of the Spirit

Scripture Focus: Joel 2:28; Romans 12:1-21; 1 Corinthians 12:1-31; 13; Ephesians 4:7-12; 1 Peter 4:10-11.

"The Holy Spirit . . . adorns us with his heavenly and divine gifts . . . frees us from sin, gives us boldness, and makes us cheerful, peaceful, pious, and holy." This statement from *The Complete Writings of Menno Simons* (pp. 495-96) is one of well over a thousand references to the Holy Spirit found in Menno's writings. Such numerous references to the Holy Spirit make it apparent that Menno could be called a Pietist before Pietism and a Methodist before John Wesley. Menno focused on a Spirit-possessed, Spirit-led, and Spirit-gifted life.

It is well to begin any discussion about the gifts of the Spirit by calling attention to *the* gift of the Spirit—life itself, which is a gift from God. The Judeo-Christian message is that our salvation, our wholeness, comes from the grace, the undeserved goodness, of God. "There are varieties of gifts, but the same Spirit" (1 Cor. 12:4). The gift of the Spirit creates unity. Gifts of the Spirit diversify and empower the church's ministry.

Paul begins the theme of 1 Corinthians 12 with the word *pneumatikon,* meaning literally spiritual things or, as translated, spiritual gifts. In most other places the word which Paul uses is *charismata,* whose literal meaning is gifts graciously given. This Greek word for gifts of grace has found its way into popular usage. The person who has a

95

mixture of charm and genius, who magnetizes others, is said to possess charisma.

Gifts—To Whom?

Most of us have tried to relate to a weeping teenager who laments, "I don't have anything going for me. I'm not good at anything. I'm ugly. I'm not popular." This kind of self-depreciation, so often found among youths, is characteristic of many Christians. In a time when many persons are rejoicing and witnessing to the gifts of the Spirit, others become depressed about their own spiritual temperatures which are not so high. And it makes some people "sick" to see others acting so well, especially when there is some suspicion that those who are so witnessing are not as well as they testify.

In the lists of the gifts of the Spirit, however, there is the assertion that "each has received a gift" (1 Pet. 4:10). There is no suggestion that gifts are reserved for the spiritually elite, who have known special kinds of experiences. "To each is given the manifestation of the Spirit for the common good" (1 Cor. 12:7). In reading Paul

---

1 Corinthians 12:4, 7-11

Now there are varieties of gifts, but the same Spirit; . . . To each is given the manifestation of the Spirit for the common good. To one is given through the Spirit the utterance of wisdom, and to another the utterance of knowledge according to the same Spirit, to another faith by the same Spirit, to another gifts of healing by the one Spirit, to another the working of miracles, to another prophecy, to another the ability to distinguish between spirits, to another various kinds of tongues, to another the interpretation of tongues. All these are inspired by one and the same Spirit, who apportions to each one individually as he wills.

1 Peter 4:10

As each has received a gift, employ it for one another, as good stewards of God's varied grace.

---

carefully, it becomes clear that the word *charismatic,* properly used, is a word to describe the entire church rather than a movement within the church. This is good news for our sense of worthlessness and weakness. For we know with Paul that "the Spirit helps us in our weakness," interceding for us when we "do not know how to pray as we ought" (Rom. 8:26). The message of the universality of the gifts is bad news, however, if we are trying to run away from responsibility.

Though each Christian receives a gift or gifts, not all have every gift. Looking at one of Paul's favorite metaphors, the body, it is obvious that all cannot be ears or feet. The body, the church, has need of each of its members. Paul follows this passage with a series of rhetorical questions: "Are all apostles? Are all prophets? Are all teachers? Do all work miracles? Do all possess gifts of healing? Do all speak with tongues? Do all interpret?" (1 Cor. 12:29-31). The answer is a resounding no!

There may be some gifts we should all desire. But it is obvious we were not all called to be apostles. It is equally obvious that not all Christians are good teachers. Since the gifts of tongues came quickly at Pentecost, many argue that this is a necessary gift as a sign that one has been fully baptized. Others reject the validity of the gift of tongues for anyone. Others point out that in the one list in which Paul seems to be prioritizing gifts, he places tongues at the bottom (1 Cor. 12:28). I have been grateful to see movement toward greater agreement concerning the gift of tongues. Growing numbers of Pentecostals and charismatics no longer believe that this gift is required of a Spirit-filled Christian, though it is still regarded as desirable and available. At the same time, increasing numbers of Christians are recognizing the validity of this gift for believers. If this mood grows, it may be more possible for those who experience the gift of tongues and those who do not to live and serve in one Spirit.

Gifts—How Many?

Our New Testament writers were joyously exercising the gifts of the Spirit more than they were carefully classifying them in order to answer the questions of future Christians. Those who have carefully studied all references to spiritual gifts have found over twenty such gifts named.

There are six lists which are often cited: general categories from 1 Peter 4:10-11, the gift of persons found in Ephesians 4:7-12, an interesting combination in Romans 12:3-8, and three lists packed into 1 Corinthians 12.

We need to use our imaginations and further Bible study to expand the number of possible gifts. We need to examine other passages as the above lists are far from exhaustive. For example, in the gospels we find a very specific gift of the Spirit promised. Since Christians will be brought before the courts, they are instructed, "Do not be anxious how you are to speak or what you are to say; for what you are to say will be given to you . . . for it is not you who speak, but the Spirit . . . speaking through you" (Matt. 10:17-20; see also Mark 13:11; Luke 12:11ff.; 21:12-15).

Another meaning for the word *comforter* that John uses for the Spirit is advocate, or attorney. If we want to gain insight concerning one of the most frequently mentioned gifts, we may need to counsel with fellow Christians such as the Berrigan brothers, who have often been gifted to share the hope which is within them before judges. This illustration suggests the interrelatedness between the gifts. For those who are given what to say in difficult situations also know the gifts of faith (special power), knowledge, wisdom, and prophecy.

Natural Endowment

In identifying the gifts of the Spirit, it may stretch our imaginations to look at an Old Testament text.

> The Lord said to Moses, "See I have called by name Bezalel . . . and filled him with the Spirit of God, with ability and intelligence, with knowledge and all craftsmanship, to devise artistic designs, to work in gold, silver, and bronze, in cutting stones for setting, and in carving wood, for work in every craft" (Exod. 31:1-5).

Here God, through Moses, calls an artist to utilize his skills for making the tent of the meeting, the ark of the covenant, and the furnishings of the tent. The special reference to the filling of the Spirit raises an intriguing question: Is a spiritual gift something bestowed supernaturally by God or is it simply a way of saying that God works through our natural abilities?

Some people would draw sharp lines between the supernatural and the natural, believing that if spiritual gifts are to be gifts of the Spirit they must defy what we name the natural order. Very likely, however, the biblical writers do not bring the same assumptions. When they speak of signs, wonders, and miracles, they are not making the sharp distinction between the natural and supernatural which we who are on this side of the scientific revolution make. Looking at the above Scripture, we could understand Bezalel as one who lacked artistic skills and then suddenly became abundantly endowed through the filling of the Spirit. Or we could interpret the filling of the Spirit as meaning that Bezalel had a lot of *charism,* a gift of the Spirit—what we today would call natural talent. The way in which we understand this, however, would not much concern the biblical writer whose main purpose was to give the credit to God.

The biblical definition of a miracle would include both what we would call natural and what we would see as supernatural. We would see a miracle in the mighty working of God through the kind of supernatural faith which could suddenly remove a mountain. Or we might discern a miracle in beholding the wonder of God in a beautiful sunset. The first might defy natural explanation; the second could be analyzed in detail by scientists. In both cases, however, the eye of the believer would behold a miracle. This question is very important in some circles. For example, in some communities the gifts of healing are an important focal point. In some instances, people have thrown away eyeglasses. In other cases, groups have decided that people who rely on the Spirit no longer need to depend upon medical science. From the types and functions of the gifts named by the New Testament writers, however, such distinctions may be artificial. In the New Testament there is no hard line between natural and spiritual gifts.

Natural gifts become spiritual if they are used to glorify God and serve others. The Spirit may gift the hands of a physician to remove a large tumor. Through the prayers of the church, the Spirit may even more

mysteriously do the same healing. A particular manifestation of a gift of the Spirit may appear to be supernatural. Or
it may appear to heighten the divine use of gifts that persons have. In either case Christians will rejoice that the empowering comes from God.

From the perspective of the Anabaptist tradition, it is
wonderful to behold that many of the gifts are people—
apostles, prophets, evangelists, pastors, and teachers.
Some of the gifts named refer more to functions. In the
New Testament, however, it is not easy to separate the two.
Some gifts refer to a capacity given to persons, such as
faith, healing, or discernment. Other gifts refer to the job
which needs to be done. Again it is often difficult to
distinguish between the gift and the job. As a practical people, we might be helped by a classification which identifies
the gifts according to function.

Gifts of Proclamation

One major cluster of gifts relates to proclaiming,
teaching, and interpreting the Word of God. *Apostles*
(Eph. 4:11; 1 Cor. 12:29) were given to the church by Christ
to be sent abroad to preach the gospel. If we limit this gift
only to the first twelve, this would be one gift no longer present today. However, Roman Catholics believe that the gift
of apostles continues in the presence of the Pope and other
bishop successors of the first twelve. And all Christians
believe that we need to adopt the style of apostolic
preaching and witness. *Evangelists* (Eph. 4:11) have been
given by the Spirit to extend the work of the apostles in
bringing the gospel to new regions. Today we also name
them as missionaries.

The *gift of teachers,* or teaching, is prominent in every
list of the gifts. Teaching is mentioned more often than the
gift of tongues in the book of Acts. In Ephesians 4:11
teachers are listed with pastors. There was an intimate
relationship between the two functions. Bishops were to be
both teachers and shepherds. In fact, the Greek word *kai*
can be rendered "and" or "that is." For this reason a better translation would be teaching shepherds, or shepherd-
ing teachers (Eph. 4:11). The gifts of knowledge and
wisdom which Paul places at the top of his list in 1 Corin-

thians 12 are, no doubt, his equivalents in this list for the gift of teaching.

The *gift of knowledge* is one of discerning the will of God. At times it may involve a disclosure of knowledge not readily available for others for the benefit of the whole congregation. Since it was important that Christian faith not be confused with the wisdom of the world, Paul might have listed the *gift of wisdom* to teach that wisdom is only true wisdom when we recognize it as a gift. Its only source is God. Whatever his purpose, Paul is not talking about speculative wisdom. Rather, the focus is on practical wisdom; the wise person is well gifted in the art of living and points to Christ crucified in teaching others how to live a Christian life.

Though these gifts of teaching, knowledge, and wisdom were highly regarded, there may be some question about how many of us should be open to these gifts. This may be what James is suggesting: "Let not many of you become teachers, my brethren, for you know that we who teach shall be judged with greater strictness" (Jas. 3:1). Whenever I, as a teacher, jump with joy or am tempted with pride, I ponder these words of the apostle James.

One of the gifts which Paul recommended most highly to both men and women was the *gift of prophecy* (1 Cor. 11:4-5; 14:1). Prophets were those who were able to share with the congregation a direct word from the Lord. Above all, prophets could help fully apply the gospel to a specific circumstance. Today, a prophet might rise to ask brothers and sisters how they are practicing hospitality to strangers. Then the prophet might give specific data about how to practice such hospitality. When a person has the gift of prophecy, such admonitions or revelations are presented in a highly inspirational and convictional way. While prophecy may be unsettling, in another sense the prophecy builds up the community.

Historians reason that this gift became less important as the canon developed. Eventually this function may have been assumed in the role of the bishop. Since prophecy represented sharing directly the word of the Lord, Paul may have been offering a possible corrective when he advised, "If your gift is prophecy, use it according to the norms and limits set by the faith" (Rom. 12:6).

This is how one should regard us,
as servants of Christ and
stewards of the mysteries of God.
1 Corinthians 4:1

Two additional gifts of proclamation are the *gift of tongues* and the *gift of interpretation of tongues.* The gift of "other tongues" given at Pentecost has been interpreted as speaking in other known languages. Whether understood as a miracle of speaking or of hearing "because each one heard them speaking in his own language" (Acts 2:6), this Pentecost experience is a dramatic reversal of the confusion of Babel. For at the earlier tower experience, different tongues divided the family of humanity. Contrary to what happened at Pentecost, the use of tongues among the Corinthians did not bring about a high quality of communication. Paul suggests that the communication occurred only with God and involved the edification of only the one person (1 Cor. 14:2, 4). For this reason Paul saw a strong need for the gift of interpretation so that there might be understanding in the entire body.

Gifts of Service

"As each has received a gift, employ it for one another, as good stewards of God's varied grace: whoever speaks, as one who utters oracles of God; whoever renders service, as one who renders it by the strength which God supplies" (1 Pet. 4:10-11).

To the gifts of proclaiming are added the gifts of service. First, Paul lists service, which in many contexts refers to those who wait on tables. To this basic function he adds the other gifts: contributing liberally, giving aid zealously, and doing acts of mercy cheerfully (Rom. 12:7-8).

It is fascinating that in the midst of all these gifts—apostles, prophets, teachers, workers of miracles, healers, and administrators—Paul sandwiches into his second list the *gift of helpers* (1 Cor. 12:28). How many sermons have you heard which featured helpers? Probably not many. This is a gift which we seldom feature, although it is certainly a needed and important gift. Helpers carry out various ministries of love and service—passing out songbooks, picking up litter, running last minute errands for the pastor or the bishop. These are all little things; yet they are so integral to the life of the community. Because almost anyone can do helping services, they are often the very things which do not get done in our congregations. Devoted helpers belong in any and every list of graced gifts.

The *gift of healing* is indispensable to any caring community. Gifted and concerned individuals, the prayers of the congregation, elders who are summoned for the rite of anointing—all manifest the gift of healing for the wholeness of sisters and brothers. Visiting a small Roman Catholic charismatic meeting, a group of us experienced with them a period of genuine rejoicing for a miraculous healing, an answer to their prayers. Through conversations after the meeting we learned more about this healing. One of the married couples who had been estranged and separated were now reconciled and together. The gift of healing is needed in all aspects of the community's life.

The *gift of faith* is another ministry of service to Christians and non-Christians alike. Some persons seem to have clear insights about the nature of God's will; they possess an unwavering conviction that God will be with us even in the face of impossible circumstances. The person thus gifted serves by modeling a depth of faith in a time of need. We often name these persons "pillars" because we can lean on their strength in times of weakness.

Then there is the ministry of the *working of miracles.* Literally the word *dunamis* means "operation or work of power." From Martin Luther to Martin Luther King, there have been persons who have served the church powerfully because of their singular effectiveness to witness with words and deeds. The working of miracles might also refer to the gift of exorcism. This gift would empower one to unfasten the grip which false gods have on people, thus opening up lives to the Spirit of Christ. For example, in order to bring ourselves to the state of mind where we want to aim missiles toward the Russians, we need to depersonalize the Russians so that they seem less human than we. One who has the gift of exorcism today could deliver us from this spirit of evil and hatred which is so strong in our culture. And this demon could be driven out only if the gifted person were able to open people to be filled with the Spirit of Jesus.

Some may think it strange that Christians are to praise God for the *gift of administrators.* Though they are necessary to guide, to manage, and to shepherd, the true function of the administrator is to serve. One of the roots of the word *administrator* is minister, which means to serve. So many good ideas are squelched with the warning, "We can't do this; we have never done it before," or "That might set a precedent." In such situations the Spirit's gift through an administrator might be to inject a "Why not?"

One of the most important gifts of service is the *gift of judgment or discernment*. The spirits need to be tested. The gifts need to be named. People need to be led in knowing how the gifts are to be used in and for the sake of the body. This gift of discernment is both one of the most neglected and one of the most important, especially in our free church heritage. The next chapter will be devoted to this one gift.

The Gift or the Way of Love

There is no question but that the charismatic gifts are gifts of God's love. It has been debated, however, whether or not love is the highest gift. Paul does interject his beautiful love chapter (1 Cor. 13) between two chapters which deal with the gifts of the Spirit. Paul concludes chapter 12 by asking the Corinthians to "be anxious for the greater gifts." He promises, then, a more excellent way. Beautifully he proceeds to show the primacy of love over the gifts: "If I have the gift of tongues of men and of angels, but have not love, I am a noisy gong. . . ."

A counter argument insists that Paul claims love to be the Way which surpasses all other ways. It is more than just a higher or the highest gift. Gifts are only useful for building up the body if they are used in love.

However one sees love, as the gift or as the Way, love is truly normative. It is the quality or gift which each and every Christian is required to have. Love, which is essential, does everything, lasts forever, and is the nature of what the Spirit is all about. The gifts must be manifest in the spirit of love if they are truly to be the gifts of the Spirit.

9.
Discerning the Gifts of the Spirit

Scripture Focus: Matthew 25:14-30; 1 Corinthians 12:10; 1 Timothy 4:14; 2 Timothy 1:6; 1 John 4:1-3.

Our heritage has nurtured a general attitude toward the gifts of the Spirit. It has advocated that *all* of life is to be lived in response to *the supreme gift* of God's love in Christ. In recent years, however, we have been asked to focus on particular gifts which have been featured by the Spirit movement. The two gifts on which much attention has centered are the gift of speaking in tongues and the gift of healing, so much so that my pride as a teacher has wanted to shout that the gifts also include the utterance of wisdom and knowledge.

As children of the Anabaptist tradition, however, we have failed to share a gift which is so basic, the gift which Paul names as "the ability to distinguish between spirits." Though this gift has been one of the most neglected, it is integral to who we are. Paul places this oft-neglected gift as number seven in his list of nine (1 Cor. 12:10). The King James version translates it as the gift of discernment. *Diakrisis* literally means "a judgment through, the ability to see through." Further, the word *ability* is more accurately translated as plural. To receive this gift is to use our abilities to know whether a spirit is truly from God or from the devil.

Discernment as Testing the Spirits

A sister who has come by a sizable amount of money for the first time in her life begins to hear voices of the Spirit instructing her to purchase $300 dresses. Through intense prayer a brother is led to make a certain business decision, resulting in millions of dollars in profits for his partnership. A preacher is directed by the Spirit to launch a crusade against gambling in his community. A youth is led to believe that a Spirit-filled life means that loving sexual relationships should not be bound by cultural norms. In these cases, as in many others, there seems to be a need for a testing of the spirits.

Father Killian McDonnell, the Catholic charismatic, writes of one of the greatest problems in the charismatic movement: "There is some uncritical acceptance of prophecy and tongues without sufficient discernment as to what comes from the Holy Spirit and what comes from the human psyche" (Michael Green, *I Believe in the Holy Spirit*, p. 192).

Jesus was disturbed by those who talked about the Lord and failed to do the will of God. To those who said: "Lord, Lord, did we not prophesy in your name, and cast out demons in your name, and do mighty works in your name?" his answer was severe: "I never knew you; depart from me, you evil doers" (Matt. 7:15-23). Paul learned about the spiritual arrogance of many enthusiastic Christians at Corinth who were eagerly manifesting the gifts of the Spirit. Paul included more than women when he cynically inquired, "Did the word of God originate with you, or are you the only ones it has reached?" (1 Cor. 14:36).

Test of the Community Gathering Around the Word

From Paul's strong language we learn that, whatever gifts we have, the Word of God does not originate with ourselves. We are not the productive source of God's revelation. Rather, we are the vehicle through which God works. We also learn from Paul that we are not the only ones to receive the Word of God. Speaking to this, Paul counseled the Corinthians: "Let two or three prophets speak, and let the others weigh what is said" (1 Cor. 14:29).

Here Paul is expressing what we have been calling the Anabaptist hermeneutic. Our gift, our prophecy, our spirit, needs to be tested with others as we gather around the faith story of our Judeo-Christian heritage. Take the matter of

107

tongues. Tongues, according to Paul and the experiences of genuine Christians, can be a vehicle for the Spirit of God. They can also be psychologically induced, as was well known in paganism. Many of the Corinthians had spoken in tongues before becoming Christians and had brought this practice with them into their newfound church. As with other gifts, this one needed the gift of discernment.

Test of Order

One of the positive things about the Christians at Corinth was that they were alive. There is evidence that many of them wanted to prophesy or speak in tongues at the same time. The women were freely speaking to one another and to their husbands. They had much to share. The aliveness obviously brought much confusion to their common life. Such provided the context for much of Paul's advice. In 1 Corinthians 14 Paul pleaded, "God is not a God of confusion but of peace." He instructed the people to take turns in speaking. He admonished, "Let all things be done for edification." He closed this intriguing chapter with the general admonition that "all things should be done decently and in order."

Some of us have participated in Spirit-filled youth conferences. Sometimes, however, there seems to be more spirit and enthusiasm than discernment. Several years ago at a large evening session at the Church of the Brethren National Youth Conference at Estes Park, Colorado, the youths seemed to be particularly "psyched up." The applause was frequent and loud. The testimonies were emotional. Where I was sitting, there were people laying on hands, casting out demons, and praying aloud, so much so that I could not hear the sermon. At this point I was almost

1 John 4:1-3

Beloved, do not believe every spirit, but test the spirits to see whether they are of God; . . . By this you know the Spirit of God; every spirit which confesses that Jesus Christ has come in the flesh is of God, and every spirit which does not confess Jesus is not of God.

led to rise and read from Paul: "God is not a God of confusion but of peace."

The Spirit does not bring disorder and irrationality; rather the Spirit gives unity and harmony. An important testing of any spirit is to discern whether it contributes to chaos or to order in the body.

Test of Communal Good

Another way to put the test of order is to ask whether a spirit or gift serves the good of the community. First Corinthians 12:7, which introduces the list of nine gifts, states the purpose: "To each is given the manifestation of a gift of the Spirit for the common good." Later in the context of speaking to the zeal of the Corinthians, Paul counseled, "So with yourselves; since you are eager for manifestations of the Spirit, strive to excel in building up the church" (1 Cor. 14:12).

The *Didache* is a second-century writing which scholars believe tells us much about the early Christians. It contains some fascinating passages on discerning the spirits. Apparently there were many wandering prophets and evangelists who claimed that they had been sent out by the churches. These travelers were given free accommodations plus a part of the tithes of a congregation and were treated with great respect. Thus arose the problem of distinguishing the true prophets from the false ones. If a prophet stayed longer than needed, it was a clear mark of his self-centeredness. The writer of the *Didache* offered rather shrewd advice in reference to finances: "If someone says in a spirit, 'Give me money or something else,' you must not listen to him; but if he tells you to give for others in need, no one should condemn him" (chapter 13).

The above second-century test might also apply to the many multimillion-dollar personal fortunes which are being made through the appeals of the electronic church. Does a gift of the Spirit serve others? Are the gifts claimed truly building up the body? As I travel around and meet Spirit-led people who are enthusiastically testifying to the gifts of the Spirit, I have two impressions. Sometimes I come away full of joy in feeling that the charismatic gifts are enlivening and reviving the total church. At other times, I come away with the desire to shake the dust off of my feet because of the great divisiveness which I found. The question of discernment is so important: Are the manifestations of the gifts truly building up the body of Christ?

Test of Christ's Spirit

Some persons have attempted to differentiate between the Spirit, God's Spirit, the Holy Spirit, the Spirit of Jesus, and the Spirit of Christ. This is more than most theologians will attempt, for most biblical scholars agree that all of these phrases point to the same reality. Their conclusion reflects Paul's affirmation "the Lord is the Spirit" (2 Cor. 3:17). It is possible to discern whether a spirit proclaims the Way of God or whether it simply reflects the rationalization of our own wishes. We can tell by discerning whether or not it resembles the Spirit of Jesus. Again the *Didache* puts it well: "However, not everybody who speaks in the spirit is a prophet, but only if he behaves like the Lord."

This christological test is important in testing natural gifts. A person may abuse or use well a high intelligence quotient. A high IQ should not be a basis for boasting; rather it remains a gift for which a person cannot take much credit. And a high IQ is not necessarily good in and of itself. It can be used for the purposes of the devil in serving the worst kind of selfish interests. Or it can be dedicated to the Lord. The same might be true of amazing and miraclelike inventions, for example, the wireless telegraph. It is great to break through communications barriers by bouncing sound waves off satellites. But if the message is "Hi, Joe" or even less significant, like reporting the odds on a winning horse, then it may not really be that great. What kind of message is conveyed? Is it to be used for the glory of God and the neighbor's good? Only then is the gift a gift of the Holy Spirit.

The well-known parable of the talents (Matt. 25:14-30) has been rightly regarded as a lesson in using whatever talents or gifts we have been given. I have participated in lengthy discussions analyzing the above point without once meditating on a most basic point in the story. We are to use whatever talents we have for the sake of the Master.

There may be a similar problem in our understanding of the parable of the last judgment (Matt. 25:31-46). We have often read this parable with the mind-set that Christians should exercise gifts of charity and mercy and do good things for others who may or may not be Christians. We make these persons the objects of Christian action. We are to so minister in order that we may be counted with the sheep instead of with the goats at the time of the great judgment. This focus may still be an important application of the parable. However, we have neglected the christological focus. Our common interpretation has made prosperous Christians the subject of the action, while Christ and his brethren have become the objects of our acts of charity. If we reverse this and make Christ and the brotherhood of the poor the subjects in the kingdom community, then our mission will be to discern how we can become more a part of this community.

Such an understanding supports an older interpretation of the parable. Throughout Matthew the phrase "the least of these" refers to weak Christians and babes in the body of Christ. This parable then was written to give comfort to them and to warn the early persecutors of the Christians. The lesson was that they would be judged according to how they treated Christians who were poor, in prison, and suffering for their faith. Translating this for our day suggests that discernment of spirits may increasingly lead us to identify more with the struggles of the poor, many of whom are already devout Bible-believing Christians. In our idolatries of nationalism and affluence, we might increasingly be the outsiders who will be judged by the way we relate to the least members of the body. However we come out in our interpretation, this parable does remind us again that spirits are to be tested according to whether they participate in the Way, the life, and the community of Jesus.

Discernment as Naming

Discernment in applying the above tests to spirits is primarily directed against the sin of self-importance. There is a need to distinguish between false and true prophets and prophecies, between what is human pride and what is divine charisma, between the gifts which tear down and those which build up, between what edifies and what confuses.

In addition, the gift of abilities of discernment is also necessary to combat the sin of self-depreciation. Like Paul we need to encourage the use of gifts and discern how best the gifts are to be used. "Having gifts that differ according to the grace given to us, let us use them" (Rom. 12:6). With love, the older elder counseled the young Timothy, "Do not neglect the gift you have, which was given to you by prophetic utterance when the elders laid their hands upon you" (1 Tim. 4:14). Exercising the gift of discernment should lead to the encouragement of all of the Timothys in our circles.

Those who exercise the gift of discernment may not only need to encourage and facilitate the use of the gifts; they may also need to name the gifts. The Bible teaches that there is power in naming and in a name. Names in the Old Testament are descriptively rich in meaning. Naming identifies, often empowers, and foretells who the person will be. Most of us have experienced a time when a person

gifted with discernment informs us that we are the one to be or to do a certain thing. And then we have experienced how difficult it is to shake off the power involved in that naming. I remember the time when my pastor first named me a future pastor. I laughed in his face and behind his back. I denied what he was saying. Later I fought vigorously against what I regarded as manipulation. But it was difficult to escape the impact of his naming me as a pastor.

In another letter to Timothy, the elder wrote, "Hence I remind you to rekindle the gift of God that is within you through the laying on of my hands: for God does not give us a spirit of timidity but a spirit of power and love and self-control" (2 Tim. 1:7). Traditionally, the laying on of hands has often accompanied the discernment or naming of gifts. In the Anabaptist tradition, one did not choose to be a communal leader. Instead one was more often named as a preacher or a deacon by the community under the guidance of the Spirit. In fact, if one aspired to leadership roles, one of the most certain ways not to be chosen was to act as if you wanted to be selected. Menno insisted that only the church has the right to commission a person to preach: "Wait until you are called of the Lord's church of the Spirit of God and are constrained by urging love."

Today, in many of our churches, individualism has held sway to the extent that we probably wait too much on personal initiative. Many are calling for a revival of the old practice of trusting the Spirit to work through the community in naming servants of the Word. The church of Jesus Christ needs a fuller exercise of the gift of abilities of discernment in order to lay hands on the very best persons for potential leadership in the body. This need not mean that individuals should be manipulated or forced to be entirely submissive to the wishes of the congregation. It could mean that corporate discernment would join individual responses in calling members to varying ministries.

At Bethany Theological Seminary, where I teach, we borrowed a practice from our sister institution, Associated Mennonite Biblical Seminaries. We call it naming the gifts. Each spring seniors spend time in naming each other's gifts. These are carefully and concisely stated. On commencement day, instead of naming honors, such as *magna cum*

114

laude, or handing out special awards of one kind or another, the gifts of each person are named as degrees are conferred.

Discerning Gifts in Congregational Life

Some are proposing that we begin practicing the same kind of discernment and naming of gifts in our congregational life. Instead of handing out sign-up sheets on which members check what they would like to do and how they would like to serve, persons would spend more time together in the naming of each other's gifts. Such discernment takes time. It might best take place in smaller groups or in classlike structures. Many gifts would be discovered which had not been recognized before. In the process, testing would likewise take place. The gift of discernment as it participates in naming would "encourage one another and build one another up" (1 Thes. 5:11).

In one congregation the naming of gifts in small groups is followed by using these gifts through special worship services. A few congregations have been daring enough to lay aside the traditional pattern of seeking persons for each slot in the organizational structure of the congregation, for example, board members, Sunday school teachers, and trustees. Instead, after spending considerable time in prayer and using the gift of discernment in naming gifts, each person's gifts are offered to one another and to the Lord. The assignments and church organization then take shape around the gifts that have been named.

Clearly the gift of discernment of gifts has an integral place in our congregational life. Imagine all of the creative possibilities which might emerge if we increasingly used the gift of discernment to call persons to faithfulness in the life of the congregation.

10.
The Spirit's Fruit

Scripture Focus: Amos 9:13-15; Luke 13:6-9; Romans 8:12-17; Galatians 5:1-26.

> I will pour out water upon the thirsty ground,
>   and streams upon the dry land;
> I will pour out my spirit upon your offspring,
>   and my blessing upon your descendants
> (Isa. 44:3)

The Spirit often comes like tongues of fire or like a mighty wind. The Spirit also speaks in a still, small voice. But there is yet another metaphor for the Spirit. In times of trial the prophets pictured the Spirit on high being poured out on us like a stream of water. The effect would be fruitfulness in the land (Isa. 32:13; Amos 9:13-15). In a similar way, the author of the fourth gospel identified the "rivers of living water" as the Spirit to be given (John 7:38-39). And in the last book of the Bible, John the Revelator continued in the same vein. As he described the New Jerusalem in his grand finale, the river of life flows from the throne of God and the Lamb down the middle of the street. On both sides there are trees which produce fruit twelve times a year (Rev. 22:1-5).

These biblical images of the Spirit as life-giving waters picture the Spirit as a nurturer of Christian growth. Through the nourishment and refreshment of the Spirit, believers show forth the fruits of a Spirit-filled life. What these Spirit fruits are and how they are evidenced in the believer's life are the issues this chapter will address.

Gifts and Fruit

The metaphor of the mighty wind points to the power of the Spirit to bring genuine change and dramatic experiences in our lives. The metaphor of rivers of water suggests the continuing, life-giving nature of the Spirit to nourish and effect growth in each person. The Pentecostal movement features the Spirit as power and mighty wind to point to the availability of the miraculous gifts. The Holiness movement calls attention to the fruit of the Spirit. Pentecostals rightly stress that powerful manifestations of the gifts did not end with the early Christians. Similarly, the Holiness emphasis on sanctification features Paul's affirmation that we presently "have the first fruits of the Spirit" (Rom. 8:23).

The fact that these are "first fruits," however, implies that there will be more and better fruit in the future. There is an eschatological goal (a moving toward the end) to the Christian life. Wesley defined his doctrine of entire sanctification or perfection in active rather than passive terms. Before we receive the second blessing, we will have known the gradual work of grace. And when we do receive it, we need to remember that we can easily lose it, that we will still make mistakes, and that we must continue to grow after the experience of perfect love.

There is another important difference between the gifts of the Spirit and the fruit of the Spirit. There are many gifts. But in Galatians the word for fruit is singular. Paul's teachings clearly indicate that no one can assume that each person has to have all the gifts. But each person should manifest the fruit of the Spirit. The Spirit gives different gifts, but the Spirit works to produce the same fruit in all. Christian growth does not consist of practicing the virtue of joy for one week and then concentrating on the virtue of peace the following week. Rather it comes through habitually living and walking in the Spirit (Gal. 5).

In the creation and fall story (Gen. 2—3) the man and the woman are forbidden to eat the fruit of the tree of the knowledge of good and evil. For when humans eat of that fruit they are tempted to take the place of God, pridefully placing human knowledge at the center of life instead of seeking God's wisdom. If, however, we live in the consciousness that knowledge flows from God through us, then it is different. Then we can bear fruit.

Fruit and Works

In the fifth chapter of Galatians the qualities of the fruit of the Spirit are preceded by a list of the works of the flesh. These manifestations of sin are *our* works. In the Bible, when evil is attributed to the demonic, it is always in a way which includes human responsibility. On the contrary, the virtues which are named are not named as works of our spirit. Rather they are identified with the fruit of the Spirit.

Paul's teaching has been referred to as "the paradox of grace." It is a paradox because it seems illogical and unfair. When we are bad, we are blamed. When we are good, God gets the credit. It did not make sense to the lad at school: "When I do well, it's because I have great teachers and good parents. When I do badly, it's my fault." When the children of Israel suffered reverses, it was because they had sinned. God called them to repentance. When they experienced good times, it was attributed to God's redeeming activity.

Such a paradox seems to defy the laws of logic. Such a paradox, however, does make good divine and human sense. We see this when we look at the opposite—the

Romans 8:15-17

For you did not receive the spirit of slavery to fall back into fear, but you have received the spirit of sonship. When we cry, "Abba! Father!" it is the Spirit himself bearing witness with our spirit that we are children of God, and if children, then heirs, heirs of God and fellow heirs with Christ, provided we suffer with him in order that we may also be glorified with him.

Galatians 5:22-23

But the fruit of the Spirit is love, joy, peace, patience, kindness, goodness, faithfulness, gentleness, self-control; against such there is no law.

Bob Taylor

person who blames everything and everybody when he or she does something wrong, but then struts and brags and takes all the credit when accomplishing anything worthy.

The sense of this paradox is found in the fact that it takes seriously both human responsibility and human dependence on God. This makes even more attractive what is basic to our Christian heritage, namely, the affirmation "Nevertheless I live, yet not I, but Christ liveth in me" (Gal. 2:20). In a mysterious and yet wonderful way, the Christian stance combines a strong sense of personal responsibility with a feeling of dependence on God.

Fruit and Christ-like Virtues
"But the fruit of the Spirit is love, joy, peace, patience, kindness, goodness, faithfulness, gentleness, self-control; against such there is no law" (Gal. 5:22). When Christians meditate on this list, they cannot help but think of the character of Christ. The qualities which the Holy Spirit seeks to give to Christ's people are the characteristics of Jesus. Sometimes it is claimed that the gospels give us the picture and the religion of Jesus. But no more beautiful description can be found of Christ-likeness than Paul's word-picture of the fruit of the Spirit.

If we are "led by the Spirit" we will become more Christ-like. We have been given a picture of life as it should be in "the light of the knowledge of the glory of God in the face of Christ" (2 Cor. 4:6). The "now/not yet" nature of "walking in the Spirit" is stated so well in a later epistle: "Beloved, we are God's children now; it does not yet appear what we shall be, but we know that when he appears we shall be like him, for we shall see him as he is" (1 John 3:2).

1. Christ-like Dispositions
Paul's first list of nine gifts in 1 Corinthians 12 has been neatly divided into three categories of three each: gifts of proclaiming, doing, and knowing. Interestingly, Galations 5:22 also names nine qualities of the fruit of the Spirit. The first three are so basic as to be regarded as the essence of Christ-like dispositions. The possession of these three—love, joy, and peace—sheds light on the last phrase in our text: "against such there is no law." For these

qualities of character point to both a freedom from sin and basic self-centeredness and a freedom to be for others in a way which is all the law requires and even more.

Love. Agape love, which loves in response to God's grace, does not ask, "What is there in it for me?" Instead, it is the quality of love which participates in the perfection to which we are called (Matt. 5:43-48). Jesus asks that our love be inclusive like the love of God, who makes the sun shine on the good and on the evil. If we only love those who love us, how are we acting any differently from tax collectors and others? The command to be perfect, as God is perfect, is meant to inspire us to allow our love to be inclusive, even as God's love is inclusive.

Joy. If we truly walk in the Spirit, Paul implies that our lives will radiate Christian joy. This is not always external jollity. Often it embodies a deep joy which nothing will be able to take away.

I have been amazed at the references to joy in the inspiring testimonies in the *Martyrs' Mirror.* One typical account tells of the execution of four brothers in A.D. 1546.

> When they were being led out to slaughter, they boldly and joyfully sang. . . . They then blessed each other, and exhorted one another to steadfastness, to be strong and of good cheer. . . . Thus all four were beheaded with the same sword and undauntedly and boldly surrendered their necks for the name of Christ (van Braght's edition, p. 475).

Peace. Shalom is the Hebrew word which provides the foundation for New Testament words for peace and salvation. It implies a strong sense of wholeness and well-being. *Shalom* comes from the knowledge that one is an adopted child of God. *Shalom* leads to a desire to live, as much as possible, in harmonious relationship with all of God's creation and creatures.

2. Christ-like Relational Virtues

The next three virtues—patience, kindness, and goodness—focus on the way we should relate to one another.

Patience. Patience is a form of love. In the classic love chapter we learn that "love suffereth long and is kind." This disposition is slow to anger, ready to forgive, and willing to bear with those who annoy us. There is a willingness to accept others as they are because God has accepted us as we are.

As a boy, I remember when Mr. Beecher scolded us for playing on his property. My father had assured us that the spot under scrutiny was a part of our lot, not Mr. Beecher's. We appealed to father to intervene and tell Mr. Beecher off. My father responded in the spirit of the patient man he was: "Mr. Beecher has a hard time at his job and at home. He has a rough life. He needs some place where he is boss. It is probably best for you to play someplace else."

Kindness. Similarly, kindness is marked by gentleness in dealing with others. Kindness goes much deeper than just a basic concern for the feelings of others. Kindness results in a positive benevolence which wishes the best for all people.

Goodness. This quality, like the others, is one of being as well as doing. In contemporary ethical theory, goodness is a characteristic of virtue ethics more than command ethics. Virtue ethics focuses on who a person is rather than on the laws by which a person lives. Nevertheless, a good person will take the initiative to translate the wish into a deed and help others in concrete, constructive ways. Thus, goodness is not concerned just with individual happiness. Goodness is sensitive to the needs of others and is compassionately involved in the agonizing problems of the twentieth century.

3. Christ-like Virtues Relating to Self

Properly coming last in the list of basic character dispositions are three virtues—faithfulness, gentleness, and self-control—which relate to ourselves.

Faithfulness. Here the virtue of faithfulness does not specifically suggest trust in God. Rather it marks a person who is trustworthy. An old saying about a Dunker may have been common in all of our denominational families: "A Dunker's word is as good as his bond." Such is a theme picked up in one of Andy and Terry Murray's songs popularizing the Brethren heritage. The song title is "Grandaddy Was a Farmer." The chorus highlights the trait of trustworthiness by singing what the miller shouted whenever Grandaddy pulled up to the millhouse with his wagon full of grain:

He's a full measure man
   He won't tell you a lie
When Cyrus rolls his wagon to the scale
   Just wave him right on by
Level on the level, signed with the shake of a hand
   Unaffected, well connected
Simple honest man.

Gentleness. This virtue is the opposite of arrogance. It is an antidote to the spirit of violence. Gentleness flows from humility and involves a willingness to submit to others when such submission is not contrary to God's will. Gentleness or meekness is not a quality of a soft, weak person. It is a virtue of the strong.

Self-Control. Literally the virtue of self-control alludes to the "power within" to rule ourselves. It implies that we are not completely at the mercy of our appetites and moods. Because it is a quality of the fruit of the Spirit, it is obviously not to be exercised in our own strength, but only in the strength of the Spirit.

We have learned that it is wrong to always repress our anger instead of finding constructive ways to express and deal with it. According to the apostle, we need to be angry and sin not. Many persons, however, have taken this insight so much to heart that they "blow up" and vent their anger whenever and wherever they feel like it. Then they suffer from feelings of guilt and remorse for having made such fools of themselves. Self-control, however, is a virtue which knows when to speak and when not to speak.

Corporate Expressions of the Fruit

In addition to the Christ-like virtues which characterize the fruitful Spirit-led life, the New Testament also gives some characteristics of a Spirit-filled community.

Howard Royer

Ephesians 5 gives one such description following the general admonitions: "Take no part in the unfruitful works of darkness" (v. 11). "And do not get drunk with wine . . . but be filled with the Spirit" (v. 18). As a result the infilling of the Spirit will overflow in "psalms, hymns and spiritual songs, singing and making melody to the Lord with all your heart, always and for everything giving thanks" (v. 19).

Witness of the Spirit and Fruit of the Spirit

"It is the Spirit himself bearing witness with our spirit that we are children of God" (Rom. 8:15). This verse became a golden text of the early Methodist movement. Converts quoted it frequently in testifying to the doctrine of assurance. How do we know whether we are in favor with God? The answer which they found in the text was that we can only know through the direct witness of the Spirit.

Before his own conversion experience, as Wesley later explained, he had the faith of a servant, of one who desired to obey God's will and serve Christ and the church. Only after his heart was strangely warmed at Aldersgate, however, could Wesley testify that he also had the faith of a son. This direct witness of the Spirit was his way of saying that he felt and knew he was loved and accepted by God. He could thus cry *Abba,* Father, with the assurance that his sins were taken away and he was saved from the law of sin and death. The Spirit offers us the assurance of God's gracious disposition toward us.

But Wesley also emphasized the indirect witness of the Spirit. The direct witness involves the meeting of God's Spirit with our spirits; the indirect witness is the presence of the fruit of the Spirit in our lives. The direct witness makes us conscious of *justification,* of God's forgiving acceptance. The indirect witness brings forth *sanctification,* the Spirit's ability to bring about Christ-like qualities in one's life.

Wesley emphasized the indirect witness through scriptural admonitions such as "Examine yourself, to see whether you are holding to your faith. Test yourselves. Do you not realize that Jesus Christ is in you?—unless indeed you fail to meet the test!" (2 Cor. 13:5). And one of the ways to meet the test is to have others discern in your walk the fruit of the Spirit.

After much struggle with self-righteousness and false testimonials on the part of zealous converts, Wesley concluded that one could have the indirect witness (the fruit of the Spirit) without the direct witness (the assurance of forgiveness and acceptance). In other words, there can be beautiful Christians whose character shows forth the fruit of the Spirit, yet who do not testify to the doctrine of assurance. Wesley was quick to add, however, that a person could not claim the direct witness of the Spirit without also having the indirect witness. In this he was saying as strongly as he could that if persons testified to the direct witness of being assured of God's forgiveness, they must also give evidence of the Spirit's fruitfulness in their lives.

Daughters and Sons, Servants and Disciples

With the strong emphasis on discipleship in our traditions, we may need to focus more strongly than we have on the personal relationship involved in the direct witness. The witness of the Spirit is the common privilege of all the children of God. We need to testify that we are daughters and sons of God as well as servants and disciples. At the same time we need not be ashamed of our contribution, which is similar to Wesley's insistence on the indirect witness of the Spirit. Our discipleship emphasis proclaims, along with Wesley, that the rivers of water which flow from the throne of God are sufficient enough and powerful enough to bear fruit in the lives of the faithful.

11.
The Spirit's Goal

Scripture Focus: Mark 16:15; Luke 4:18-21; John 4:19-21; Acts.

Why did or does the Spirit come? We have seen that the Spirit comes to give life, to proclaim tidings of good news in the midst of bad news. The Spirit comes to bring understanding and light to the words of Scripture. The Spirit comes to enable the Word, Jesus Christ, to live in and through us. We have seen that the Spirit's fruit creates a quality of life in Christians which otherwise they would not know. The Spirit gives power and gifts in order that the meek and powerless will inherit the earth. We have seen how the Spirit builds up the body so that believers know a quality of fellowship which the world cannot give or take away. But above all, the goal of the Spirit is to send us out as witnesses, to empower us to be participants in the coming of the kingdom. "Go into all the world and preach the gospel to all creation" (Mark 16:15).

The Spirit's Manifestations
One way to think of God's nature and intentions is through the doctrine of the trinity. It is never easy to simplify the notion of One in Three and Three in One. Yet God's ways are not our ways. There will always be a sense of mystery as we sing "blessed trinity."

Here we will look at an interpretation, not the interpretation, of the trinity. We will name this a historical view

127

because it simply relates how the God story happened.

The people of Israel were strict monotheists. They believed only in Yawheh, whose holiness was so great that the name could not be pronounced and whose nature was too mysterious to be molded into any image. Still, Yahweh acted mightily for their sake and for the good of the world. To these people came a man who lived among them. After being with him, they were convinced that Yahweh's nature was clearer. They were certain that somehow Yahweh was with them in and through this man. But this manifestation was not something entirely different. The God of Jesus Christ was the same God as the God of Abraham.

Though this story seemed tragically finished with the death of Jesus on the cross, something further happened. The people experienced that Jesus was still alive and with them. His Spirit came in a powerful way on the day of Pentecost. Again, this was not a different God; rather, the same God was bringing power and life anew.

And yet, even as we think of the one God being manifest in these three events, we need also to think of all three manifestations somehow being present in each event. In the Genesis story, the first Person of the trinity was manifest as the Spirit, hovering over the deep waters to create order out of chaos and to give humanity the breath of life. Later, this same Spirit brought rattling and new life to the valley of dry bones (Ezek. 37). Similarly, in the birth narratives about the second Person, there is a full measure of the Spirit. The persons close to Mary— Zechariah, Elizabeth, and John—were

Mark 16:15
And he said to them, "Go into all the world and preach the gospel to the whole creation."

Acts 1:8
"But you shall receive power when the Holy Spirit has come upon you; and you shall be my witnesses in Jerusalem and in all Judea and Samaria and to the end of the earth."

all filled with the Holy Spirit. A new promised, powerful expression of the Spirit, which we name the third Person, appeared on another birthday, that of the Christian church. Those assembled experienced new power and life with the coming of a mighty wind and tongues of fire. Thus we see in the biblical witness the close interrelatedness of these three manifestations.

Back to the original question. What was the purpose behind this powerful threefold manifestation of the Spirit? God's purposes become obvious as the Genesis story unfolds. God, through Abraham, called out a people for a purpose (Gen. 12). The covenant included both a command and a promise. The command was to get out "to the land that I will show you." The promise was in the form of a blessing: "And I will bless you . . . so that you will be a blessing . . . and by you all the families of the earth will be blessed" (vv. 1-3).

In the birth, the temptation, and the baptism of Jesus, the same promise is fulfilled. As the Spirit descended at his baptism, Jesus was "anointed to preach good news" (Luke 4:18), equipped and given power for his public ministry. With the great outpouring of the Holy Spirit at Pentecost, the apostles were given power to be sent forth in mission. The mission to the Gentiles and to the nations was nothing other than the continuation of the ministry of Jesus and the fulfillment of the promise to Abraham to be witnesses to and a blessing for all the peoples of the earth.

Missionary Spirit

Michael Green has stated it well: The Comforter does not come to make us comfortable but to make us missionaries (*I Believe in the Holy Spirit*, p. 58). A Greek synonym for comforter is advocate. In the story of the first Christians, the Spirit often gave words so that Christians could be advocates in witnessing boldly to the world. Ever since then, periods of powerful manifestations of the Holy Spirit have been accompanied by missionary activity. The monastic movement in some ways represented a prayer meeting in retreat from the world. Yet from monasticism came missionaries who led in winning the northern barbarians for Christ—Patrick in Ireland, Martin in France, and Boniface in Germany.

Bob Taylor

In desiring to restore anew the Spirit-filled consciousness of the early Christians, many sixteenth-century Anabaptists adopted the traveling and letter-writing style of the
apostles. No words of the Master were given more serious
attention than the Great Commission. These early Anabaptists saw the Great Commission as a command for each and
every Christian. Most mainline Reformers interpreted the
command to "go into all the world" as having been finished
by the apostles and thus no longer speaking to the parish
system of their day. Not until a century and a half later did
Pietism, empowered by a Holy Spirit renewal, bring about a
missionary movement within the state churches. The doctrine of the Spirit was basic to Wesley's theology and activity, and it became the seedbed for widespread revivals and
the extension of evangelical Christianity.

Following the American revolution, Methodist-like
revivals swept across the American frontier like prairie
wildfire. In the twentieth century, Pentecostalism has been
the fastest growing grass-roots movement and has been
named as the powerful third force within Christendom.

Thus we see that historically, evangelism and missions have flourished whenever there has been a revival of
the doctrine of the Holy Spirit. Clearly the Spirit's purpose
has been "to send forth."

Universal Spirit

"The hour is coming when neither on this mountain
nor in Jerusalem will you worship. . . . God is spirit, and
those who worship him must worship in spirit and truth"
(John 4:19-24). This text has often been used to contrast in-
sincere exterior worship with authentic interior worship.
Though partially valid, this interpretation could be
misleading. The author does not have in mind something
entirely "spiritual" in the sense of that which cannot be
seen, heard, or sensed. According to John, to "worship in
spirit and in truth" means to worship an incarnational em-
bodiment of God, to worship the person of Jesus himself.
Geographic institutions, such as the Jerusalem temple and
Mount Gerizim, have been replaced. All loyalties, including
cultic and nationalistic loyalties, are superseded by the
universal appeal and message of Jesus.

131

Along with the Great Commission another favorite text of the early Anabaptists was Psalm 24. This psalm begins with the affirmation that "the earth is the Lord's and the fulness thereof, the world and those who dwell therein." These poor and persecuted pilgrims, though in conflict with worldly powers, still showed in their lives a deep love for God's earth and all of God's people. They gave highest priority to allegiance to Jesus Christ, rather than allegiance to tribal, ethnic, and nationalistic loyalties. This highest priority of allegiance to Jesus Christ has been one of the Anabaptists' greatest contributions to Christendom.

Of like significance has been the Anabaptist conviction that the welfare of all people is more important than the narrow interests of one group or one nation. This truth was grounded in the Pentecost experience of the first Christians. The disciples, who had thought of the kingdom in more narrow geographic and national terms, were led to accept the three thousand who were baptized and commissioned to preach the gospel to the Gentiles.

Ironically, it was this same universal concern for all people, expressed by my Sunday school teachers, which led to my first deep feeling on nonconformity. Many people were first introduced to this doctrine of noncomformity when they were admonished to be different in dress, in speech, in personal habits. During World War II some of this teaching did filter through to me. Primarily, however, what was more scandalous was the teaching that we should love all people. In the city where I grew up, the predominant mood toward the Japanese and the Germans, our "enemies" at that time, was one of intense hatred. It was the universal teaching about love for all, even enemies, which first personally involved me in the scandal of nonconformity.

This experience of mine illustrates how a love for all, even for enemies, need not be separated from rootedness in community. Similarly, on the day of Pentecost the Spirit's fruit resulted in both the adding of three thousand souls and also devotion to the apostles' teaching, fellowship, the breaking of bread, and prayers (Acts 2:41-42).

Mission at home is consistent with mission abroad. The Spirit who nurtures also sends. My mother was once

confronted by a sister who asked why she was quilting for people overseas when there was so much need at home. My mother replied that her experience showed that persons who were interested in the needs of people in other countries were often the very persons concerned about the needs of their close neighbors. It is the same Spirit who nurtures at home and sends forth in mission.

Sending Spirit

"But you shall receive power when the Holy Spirit has come upon you; and you shall be my witnesses in Jerusalem and in all Judea and Samaria and to the end of the earth" (Acts 1:8). We have seen that it is the Spirit who stamps the mark of mission on the church. The root word for apostle is "sent one." Other than in the birth narratives, whenever Matthew, Mark, or Luke writes of someone having the Spirit, it is in relation to mission. For example, when the Gospel of Matthew speaks of the disciples having the Spirit, it is related to mission (Matt. 10:20).

133

The intimate relationship between baptism and mission has been neglected in our teaching. Often people wonder why Jesus, who was without sin, needed to be baptized. He was not baptized for remission of sins. The voice of the Spirit commissioned Jesus for loving service. His public ministry stood in the sign of the Spirit. Jesus' baptism by water and by Spirit marked the end of his period of isolation and the beginning of his public ministry. Through his baptism in the muddy waters of the Jordan, Jesus repudiated the cultic sense of being saved from this world which mystery religions espoused. Jesus' baptism was, rather, a powerful act of his sense of solidarity with sinners and the beginning of his public mission.

In the Believers' Church tradition, the baptism of Jesus needs to again become more of a major focus. Understanding baptism as ordination for public ministry may be only one of many meanings, but it is a basic meaning. In our heritage, baptism and confirmation coincide through the close association we have generally maintained between water and Spirit baptism. Confirmation involves the commissioning of a believer to become a part of the mission of the church. Such a view can be seen in a passage from *Apology* of Alexander Mack Jr., the son of one of the founders of the Church of the Brethren:

> Just as the Chief High Priest pledged himself to the Father through His baptism to make the entire rebelling creation subject to Him, so all of His followers with their baptism have pledged themselves by oath to Him to assist Him in this task. That is why Peter calls them a royal priesthood (Donald Durnbaugh, *The Brethren in Colonial America,* p. 510).

We have seen how the Anabaptists were among the first to make the Great Commission binding upon all members. Something of their zeal is reflected in the quote found in *The Origins of Sectarian Protestantism* by Franklin Littell (p. 111): "For Christ didn't say to his disciples: go forth and celebrate the Mass, but go forth and preach the Gospel." Contrary to many general impressions today, the

134

first generation of Hutterite communities provided a home base for ardent missionary activity. Itinerant preachers, such as Hans Hut, reasoned that since preaching preceded faith and baptism, proclaiming the gospel should be high on any list of priorities in discipleship. Such zeal accounted for the widespread growth of the sixteenth-century radical movement. Had it not been for the systematic extermination of leadership in many places, Anabaptism may well have become the dominant movement in many lands where the spirit of reformation was strong.

The word *witness,* which appears thirty times in the book of Acts, became a favorite word among the sixteenth-century radicals. Witness describes both their martyr faith and their missionary stance. They were not "saving souls" as much as they were witnessing to the power, the forgiveness, and the Way of Christ. They witnessed; the Spirit converted. This style was especially important in light of the prevailing compulsion in matters of faith and practice in the state churches. The Anabaptists did not add members by infant baptism or by forcing belief at the point of the sword. Rather they felt that the Spirit convicted through the voluntary response of hearers to the contagious witness of a loving community. Since they rejected infant baptism, the Anabaptists then needed to adopt a missionary posture in relation to their own children.

Sovereign Spirit

A prominent British clergyman publicly related the story of one of his trips to London. It had been a grueling week. He rushed to catch the bus, barely had time to purchase a ticket, and was the last one in a long line to squeeze inside. Working his way toward the back of the bus, he luckily stood by a seat which was vacated at the first stop. In telling this story, he praised God for the leading of the Spirit on that difficult day. A parishioner among his hearers reacted somewhat skeptically. He had been on that same bus and had given up his seat to an old woman who also had barely caught the bus. And he had, quite frankly, been miserable the entire trip.

This story illustrates a very common misuse of the consciousness of the Spirit's presence. Often there is an inclination to identify the work of the Spirit with a person's own comforts and successes. In the above story, is the Spirit's presence to be identified with personal comfort or with an act of helpfulness? What about those persons left standing? Was God less concerned about them? Does God play favorites?

Dietrich Bonhoeffer's analysis of cheap grace is frequently quoted. He defined cheap grace as justification of sin without justification of the sinner. This is illustrated by a person who out of one side of the mouth confesses that all our righteousness is but as filthy rags and out of the other side says: "They are only poor because they are lazy. If they were hard-working, industrious, good people like me, they would prosper." Cheap grace is praying that God will forgive our sins, but not, however, as we forgive others. Such teaching centers more on what the Spirit can do for us than on how we might participate in the Spirit's goals.

Similarly Bonhoeffer contrasted what he called the god of religion with the God of the Bible. The *deus ex machina* is the popular god who works like a machine in responding to our wishes and needs. The God of the Bible, however, calls us to participate in God's suffering for the sins of the world.

Some may feel that Bonhoeffer's thought represents more of a corrective than the whole story. His is an important biblical emphasis for our era, however, when "pop religion" caters to people's basic selfish interests. Popular religion focuses on saving our lives. The gospel teaching warns that "whoever would save his life will lose it, and whoever loses his life for my sake will find it" (Matt. 16:25). And rather than the popular "Seek first physical health, peace of mind, and worldly success," the teaching of our Lord is quite specific: "Seek first God's kingdom and his righteousness and all these things shall be yours as well" (6:33).

We need to remember that the Spirit remains sovereign.The Spirit refuses to be domesticated for popular consumption or manipulated for our purposes. The Spirit's goal is nothing other than to continue the purpose of Christ's coming. God sent Christ not to condemn the world but that the world might be redeemed (John 3:17). The Holy Spirit is not to be confined to the narrow straits of Jewish or American respectability.

We have discovered that it is impossible to find a tidy doctrine of the Spirit. The Spirit always retains an unpredictable, mysterious otherness. And yet, the biblical view suggests strongly that whenever there is a choice between serving selfish interests and serving kingdom goals, the Spirit is bent on sending the people of Jesus in mission.

Some Christians who testify to a Spirit-baptism use gifts and bear fruit in such a way as to reveal a genuine experience. From my perspective, however, some persons so sharply differentiate between their life before Spirit-baptism and their life afterwards that they deny some basics of the Christian Way. I am thinking of persons in the peace church tradition who look at their earlier efforts in peacemaking and service as a part of their liberal past. Their charismatic experience, instead of empowering their peacemaking concerns, has led them to turn their backs on the call to be peacemakers.

We need to see the power of the Spirit coming together with the goal of the Spirit. We live in an era in which many persons have the right vision of what the kingdom of peace and justice might be, yet lack the motivation and power to be deeply committed to the kingdom coming. Others testify that they are filled with the power of the Spirit or turned on to Jesus, yet have a very limited view of the Spirit's purpose. It is wonderful, therefore, to behold faith communities which are overcoming the barriers between those persons who have power without a focus and those persons who have a sense of mission without power.

Hospitable, Compassionate, and Sent

Spirit-led people will be a hospitable people, opening their doors and hearts to the prisoner, to the stranger, and to other sisters and brothers of Jesus. Spirit-led people will be compassionate like the One who was so moved by the sins of the people that he wept over Jerusalem because she knew not the things that make for peace. Spirit-led people will be a sent people, preaching the gospel to all people.

12.
The Spirit and
the Sojourner

Scripture Focus: Hebrews 11—12.

The Spirit commands "go . . . preach . . . teach . . . baptize." Those who are so sent may share wonderful manifestations of the work of the Spirit and may participate in a bountiful harvest of the first fruits of the kingdom. On the other hand, however, they may very well be rebuked, rejected, imprisoned, or crucified. One needs only to read church histories and the stories of martyrs to know this. For example, a famous missionary gathering of Anabaptist leaders, who met at Augsburg in 1527, later became known as the Martyr Synod. Only two or three of those who participated in this meeting survived as long as five years to assess their efforts. The others joined countless numbers of sisters and brothers who were tortured in various ways— having their tongues cut out, tied in sacks and drowned, beheaded with a swing of the sword, or tied to the stake and burned.

Our difficulty today in understanding their experience would be less if we would open the *Martyrs' Mirror* and read the accounts of these faithful pilgrims. We would soon understand why they so quickly identified with certain biblical names for the people of God, for they too lived as sojourners, strangers, aliens, exiles, and pilgrims.

Sojourners and Exiles for Christ

From numerous biblical images for the Spirit, certain

138

images spoke powerfully to these sixteenth-century pilgrims. Among these are words which describe the work of the Spirit as "earnest," "adoption," "first fruits," and "seal." The last metaphor will serve as an example which relates the Spirit with sojourning.

The Ephesians are told that having received the gospel they are "in Christ" and "sealed" with the Holy Spirit (Eph. 1:13). "Seal" is a property word. It speaks of belonging. The Holy Spirit brands us to identify that we belong to Jesus just as the brand on a sheep identifies its master. Though we are not certain exactly what the author had in mind, second-century Christians interpreted the seal as referring to baptism.

This same application became meaningful also in the sixteenth century. The Anabaptists believed that through baptism they were sealed or stamped as belonging to Jesus rather than to the powers and principalities. We sometimes have criticized our spiritual ancestors for writing and speaking so much about baptism. For them, however, baptism was literally a matter of life and death. Life in Christ meant a possible death sentence from the authorities who regarded their baptism as illegal rebaptism. Baptism for them as well as for us sealed a relationship to Christ and to his body.

Unlike its meaning in the contemporary church, however, baptism for the Anabaptists meant a position of radical nonconformity to culture. Baptism meant an entirely different understanding of the relationship of the Christian to the state. Because of persecution many early Anabaptists were forced to wander as pilgrims, seeking and giving strength in little bands of the faithful. As persecution grew more savage, hundreds of families took to the road, becoming sojourners and exiles for Christ.

Today, most of us are so comfortably settled that we are not much aware of the genuine interest that other persons have in Anabaptism. This interest stems, as it did in the sixteenth century, from the growing realization that to be Christian is to be in radical tension with our culture. People are realizing that commitment to the Way of Christ cannot be reconciled to the popular infatuation with violence, the desire to be first in producing weapons of death, and the materialism which leads to false priorities for us and injustice for others. Increasingly Christians who want to participate in kingdom promises are feeling more like pilgrims, strangers, and sojourners.

Sojourners—In the Land but Not of the Land

Hebrews 11—12 defines profoundly what it means to be pilgrims, strangers, and sojourners. In the great faith chapter of the Bible, Abraham is held up as a model of faithfulness. "By faith he sojourned in the land of promise, as in a foreign land, living in tents with Isaac and Jacob, heirs with him of the same promise" (Heb. 11:9). The word *sojourner* literally means resident alien. Early in the story Abraham was sent to a land which was promised his descendants but in which he lived like an alien. Because this very land was promised to him, he could endure faithfully and patiently as a wandering Aramean.

The word *pilgrim* is not all that different from *sojourner* except that it implies "being on the way." When the children of Abraham later settled more permanently in the land, they were frequently reminded that because their fathers were wandering Arameans they should grant hospitality and justice to the sojourners in their midst. The same should probably be said more often to the inheritors of the peace church tradition. "Because your fathers were 'yellow' pacifists and emigrants coming to our land to seek special favors, you should be more tolerant of farm workers, the unemployed, the refugees, and other victims of massive economic systems whether they be capitalist or communist."

Hebrews 11:8-10

By faith Abraham obeyed when he was called to go out to a place which he was to receive as an inheritance; and he went out, not knowing where he was to go. By faith he sojourned in the land of promise, as in a foreign land, living in tents with Isaac and Jacob, heirs with him of the same promise. For he looked forward to the city which has foundations, whose builder and maker is God.

In holding up Abraham's faith and example, the author of Hebrews was suggesting that Christians do not reside as permanent residents. Since their citizenship is elsewhere, Christians are in the world but not of it. They are to take their orders, not from the standard-bearers of the world but from the pioneer and perfector of the faith.

In his excellent book *The Outward Bound,* Vernard Eller describes the pilgrim church as a *caravan church.* The caravan church is contrasted to the commissary church, which sees itself as an institution stocked by God with a supply of heavenly graces: "Bible truths, correct theology and the sacraments." In the commissary church, the clerical proprietors are authorized to disburse the goods to the customers. On the contrary, the caravan church "is a group of people banded together to make common cause in seeking a common destination" (p. 12). The commissary church is concerned with success; it strives to be something. It is preoccupied with security, it wants to be somewhere. The pilgrim people who constitute the caravan church are concerned with getting somewhere. They desire that their steps be in the direction of the kingdom coming.

It is important to keep in mind that the pilgrim does not despise the land through which he or she is traveling. Though pilgrims take orders from beyond, these orders are for the good of the land where the pilgrim resides. The posture of the pilgrim is not one of running away from the world; rather, the pilgrim has a divine vision of what the world might become. Pilgrims walk with a purpose. Because they derive their marching orders from the Spirit, pilgrims can march joyously and relate to others lovingly.

The peace church tradition knows a heritage which accents both "love not the world or the things in the world" and "love the world because God loved the world." Conformity to the mind of Christ does not lead us to love the perverted values, sick priorities, degenerate habits, and false nationalistic idols of our culture. At the same time, peace churches have affirmed the world as they fostered a proper stewardship and love of God's good earth, modeled a mutual caring and sharing in life together, and shared a love so universal that it includes enemies. Sojourners love the strangers in the land at the same time they feel like strangers themselves. In summary, sojourners do not love the world as it is, because they love it so much that they would like for it to become what God wants it to be.

Sojourners—Holding to the Promises

In the faith chapter we learn why Abraham was a sojourner or pilgrim: "For he looked forward to a city which has foundations, whose builder and maker is God" (Heb. 11:10). Faith placed Abraham in a large place from which he could view the pilgrimage from the perspective of God. For this reason Abraham and his people could walk, standing firmly on the promises of God. Their faith was in the promise rather than in what appeared to be obvious. Because she trusted God's promise for their future, Sarah, by faith, "received power to conceive, even when she was past the age" (11:11). And it was only by faith that Abraham could offer up this same and only son in sacrifice with the assurance that somehow God's promises would work out. By faith we can believe in the possibility of what appears to be impossible.

In the field of biblical studies there is a keen interest in what is called the apocalyptic. This word, which literally means unveiling or revelation, refers to a special body of literature which appeared between the Testaments. The colorful visionary language of apocalyptic literature also found its way into the book of Daniel, the little apocalypse in Mark 13, and the book of Revelation. In addition many scholars believe that apocalypticism was the background out of which most New Testament writers formulated their messages of hope. For apocalyptic hope promises that newness can emerge out of the death of the old. As in the case of Daniel and Revelation, the apocalyptic message was written to bring encouragement and comfort to those facing difficult times. It proclaimed that, in spite of bitter persecution, God still rules and God's way will triumph.

Apocalyptic hope has been defined as "a hope in spite of." In spite of the way history seems to be moving, Christians can hold fast to the promises of God. In contrast, prophetic hope was often based on a more positive reading of history. In discerning God's faithfulness in the past, the prophets knew that God would be faithful in the future. Apocalyptic hope is more radical. In spite of a more pessimistic reading of the movement of history, we can still live with the expectancy of the breaking in of the radically new.

For thirty years I have been working in the peace movement. What has kept me involved for this period of time? If I had to depend for my inspiration on what has been accomplished, I would have been burned out long ago. The arms race seems more out of control now than ever before. The hope which motivates me can only be described as apocalyptic. In spite of the continuing race toward holocaust, in spite of the growing infatuation with and faith in violence, I live with the hope that something new and unexpected might break into history. I have been influenced by the Quakers who seem to me to be the charismatics of the peace movement. They refuse to abandon their faith that the Spirit can powerfully break in anew to bring the kingdom.

Jesus faced some of the same questions, for he too lived in an apocalyptic atmosphere. Then, even as today, when history seemed to be failing, people looked for all kinds of signs and schemes about the last days. Jesus was harder on these people than we dare to be or have a right to be. He said, "An evil and adulterous generation seeks for a sign, but no sign shall be given to it except the sign of Jonah" (Matt. 16:4). What is this sign of Jonah? It may very well be the sign which points to the power of God to convert the worst of evildoers, even the citizens of Nineveh. Only an unlikely sojourner like Jonah could have done that. It is the apocalyptic hope that even the most wicked power centers of our day (dare we say Moscow or Washington?) might repent and turn around. Only by faith in the promises of God can contemporary pilgrims engage in the foolishness of preaching the gospel of repentance to a death-prone world.

Sojourners—Walking by Faith

Pilgrims walk, standing on the promises of God; nevertheless, they cannot know absolutely or prove everything. Their strong conviction is "of things not seen" (Heb. 11:1). Though some Christians believe they are able to describe exactly the furniture of heaven and the temperature of hell, the apostle Paul was more modest. He wrote that we only "know in part," that "our knowledge is imperfect" and that "we see in a mirror dimly" (1 Cor. 13). Noah acted in response to God's promises but on the basis of "events as yet unseen" (Heb. 11:7).

Such is the case with all strong convictions. We may profess great love for another person; it is difficult, however, to prove rationally or demonstrate conclusively the basis of our conviction. In many areas we walk by faith more than by sight. This is not to say, however, that our faith should not seek greater wisdom and understanding.

Pilgrims are freed for greater faithfulness in spite of the consequences. Their stance makes possible an old Christian testimony: "I would rather fail in a cause which will ultimately triumph than be successful in a cause which is destined to fail." As Christians we do not have to wait for the guarantee that others will be loving before we begin to love. Abraham heeded the call, not because he could see that everything would work out, but because he held fast to the promise.

There have been times when I calculated exactly what would happen if I acted in a particular way. I just knew that people would be turned off by my Christian testimony. To my surprise, however, there were responses I had not expected, and the results were much different from what I had anticipated. Because the stance of the pilgrim is to be faithful more than it is to be successful, the pilgrim can be open to the unexpected, the coming of the new. Success might be given. But failure will be interpreted in the light of the ultimate victory of resurrection faith.

Again, it needs to be said that the sojourner's status of citizenship in another commonwealth does not negate the possibility of serving in the place he or she is passing through. Abraham's neighbors were enriched by the presence of the wandering stranger in their midst. So, too, when we are not calculating how to get along successfully, we are freed from those priorities which make it difficult to be for the world. The procession of saints through the centuries illustrates well that otherworldliness need not negate loving service to the world. For example, when Francis of Assisi left his affluent life as a young knight, he was freed to become a minister of reconciliation in his world.

144

"I shall remain a wanderer until mankind has learned the way of peace, walking until I am given shelter and fasting until I am given food."
— *Peace Pilgrim*

The picture of a pilgrim, who walks by faith rather than by sight in holding fast to the promises of God, is expressed beautifully in an early Christian apology, *Letter to Diognetus,* written in the second century:

> Christians cannot be distinguished from the rest of the human race by country or language or customs. . . . Although they live in Greek and barbarian cities alike, as each man's lot has been cast, and follow the customs of the country in clothing and food and other matters of daily living, at the same time they give proof of the remarkable and admittedly extraordinary constitution of their own commonwealth. They live in their own countries, but only as aliens. They have a share in everything as citizens, and endure everything as foreigners. Every foreign land is their fatherland, and yet for them every fatherland is a foreign land. They marry, like everyone else, and they beget children, but they do not cast off their offspring. They share their board with each other, but not their marriage bed. . . . They love all men, and by all men are persecuted. . . . [In short] Christians dwell in the world, but do not belong to the world (Cyril C. Richardson ed., Library of Christian Classics, Vol. 1, *Early Christian Fathers,* pp. 213-14).

Sojourners—Now, but Not Yet

In this classic description of the early Christians, one truth becomes clear. Though their citizenship is in heaven and they live on earth as aliens, Christians can begin to live now according to the "extraordinary constitution of their own commonwealth." They are already enjoying the privileges of their heavenly citizenship. In the Hebrew definition of faith, commentators point out that another word for assurance is title-deed. Faith, therefore, is the title-deed we have of things hoped for. This suggests that we can begin to possess now what has been promised.

This same meaning is implied by other metaphors for the Spirit. One of these is "earnest," a word of commerce which refers to a down payment or first installment. Or in the Revised Standard Version it is translated as a guarantee. Paul writes that the Spirit is the guarantee which is given by God (2 Cor. 5:5). As pilgrims, we receive the Spirit as the part of the future we have in the present. We can look forward to a greater gift and fuller citizenship at the same time we experience the reality of the present gift.

Another metaphor, meaningful for those who are farmers at heart, is the designation of the Spirit as "first fruits" (Rom. 8:23). As pilgrims on our way we can begin to taste the first fruits of what the Spirit promises in the later fullness of the harvest. All of these metaphors define the people of God as treading the highways to Zion. By virtue of God's sure promise, they have already arrived in some aspects of their lives. In another real sense, however, they have not yet arrived.

The "now/not yet" reality is helpful in describing the nature of apocalyptic hope. In the New Testament we learn that the kingdom is both present and future. We know that the perfect kingdom of peace, righteousness, and justice is ahead, though it will not come until the fullness of God's time. We also have been promised a taste of some of the first fruits of the kingdom now. The kingdom, therefore, is both now and not yet. Whenever we identify any of our own causes or institutions with the kingdom, we need to remember that God's kingdom judges our own attempts to build the kingdom on earth. Whenever we meet those who want to place the kingdom entirely in the future, we need to remember the instruction to pray, "Thy kingdom come, on earth, now." Some "pop" apocalypticists believe that since the kingdom will not arrive until Jesus returns to set it up, the Sermon on the Mount is not for us. It is only for the people who will be gathered to live in the millenial kingdom. The "now/not yet" reality is helpful to correct this unbiblical teaching. For the future kingdom can begin now to break into our lives and into the world as a powerful force.

This "now/not yet" hope was dramatized in my childhood around the love feast tables. I puzzled over what the elders were talking about when they pointed to that future messianic banquet where in perfect fellowship we would rest our heads on Abraham's bosom. The more I think about it, the more I believe they were saying, "Brothers and sisters, we do not have perfect love around these tables. We are not the kind of community God wants. But we do meet in joy as we experience a foretaste of the kind of love and peace which God desires for the entire world and which God has promised in the kingdom coming."

The oft-told story of the young Mennonite in Russia dramatizes the same truth. Appearing as a conscientious objector before his judge, he was admonished, "Your way is only for the kingdom. Don't you realize that the kingdom has not yet come?" The answer was as simple as it was profound: "The kingdom may not have come for you, judge, or for Russia. But it has come for me, and I must begin to live now as if it has."

A Twentieth-Century Sojourner

As I write at the end of July 1981, I receive a church newsletter in memory of Peace Pilgrim. This sister provides a beautiful example of a sojourner who was filled with the Spirit. A few weeks ago she was killed near Knox, Indiana. The car in which she was riding was hit by another vehicle which crossed the center line. I could not help but be impressed by the fact that at the very moment I was struggling with what to say about the meaning of sojourners, I was asked to remember a twentieth-century pilgrim.

In 1953, Peace Pilgrim began a prayer walk for peace. Divesting herself of all belongings and taking only what could be placed in the pockets of her tunic, she began a pilgrimage which was to cover more than 25,000 miles. Her vow was, "I shall remain a wanderer until mankind has learned the Way of Peace, walking until I am given shelter and fasting until I am given food." She dramatized that she was not a citizen in this world; yet through her the Spirit was powerfully present in the lives of many. We were privileged to have her in our home on a couple of occasions. I did not completely agree with her philosophically. Her lifestyle may not be advisable for many. But I do want to offer thanks for one who provided a contemporary example of a pilgrim for the Prince of Peace. We will miss her radiant presence and powerful testimony. We rejoice that she walked among us and is now at home.

13.
Themes From Romans 8

Scripture Focus: Romans 8:1-39; 1 Corinthians 1:18-31; 2:1-16; Galatians 5.

One vacation Bible school of my childhood is memorable because of the bright ribbon I received as a part of the closing exercises. I had memorized a sizable number of biblical passages which were named "beauty spots" by our teachers. Romans 8 was not one of them, but it should be for any similar project for adults!

Romans 8 is one of the great chapters of the Bible. It describes the Christian life: a life of freedom, a life which shares in Christ's suffering, a life of hope, of prayer, of assurance, and of victory over all trials and enemies. Above all, Romans 8 is about life in the Spirit. There is not a chapter in the Bible which says more about the Spirit than this one. It does not focus on who and why the Spirit *is* as much as on what the Spirit *does.* It calls for meditation rather than cool analysis. If you need to choose between reading Romans 8 and this interpretative chapter, read thoughtfully and prayerfully Paul's powerful testimony to the Romans.

I have already quoted from the chapter several times. In his commentary on the book of Romans, Karl Barth writes over fifty pages on this chapter alone, and from my humble perspective, even then he neglects some important themes. Marcus Loane writes an entire book, *The Hope of Glory,* commenting on this one chapter.

After reading these and others, I could now use Paul's themes to summarize all I have written about the Spirit. Or I could present Paul's doctrine of the Spirit in some systematic fashion. There are so many golden texts and great themes. For example, Paul introduces the notion of predestination, and it is tempting to use this as an opportunity to offer my ideas on this issue. Instead, I will focus on two basic underlying themes in Romans 8: the flesh and Spirit dualism, and the theology of glory and the theology of the cross.

Flesh and Spirit Dualism

One of Paul's basic purposes in Romans 8 is to contrast life according to the flesh with life in the Spirit. This contrast has led many persons to read Paul through the eyes of a flesh-spirit dualism. A simple dictionary definition explains dualism as the belief that persons are divided into two parts, body and soul. The body is equated with the flesh. In philosophy the soul is often identified with the mind. In religious circles the soul is frequently defined as the heart or as the substance of the divine which is found in the creature. An even more complicated division of a person has been a threefold division of body, soul, and spirit. For the most part, however, the traditional Jewish stance refused to make such distinctions. For the Old Testament writers the soul was the whole person—body and mind. When we read that a number of souls journeyed to Egypt,

Romans 8:28, 35, 37-38

We know that in everything God works for good with those who love him, who are called according to his purpose. . . . Who shall separate us from the love of Christ? Shall tribulation, or distress, or persecution, or famine, or nakedness, or peril, or sword? . . . No, in all these things we are more than conquerors through him who loved us. For I am sure that neither death, nor life, nor angels, nor principalities, nor things present, nor things to come, nor powers, nor height, nor depth, nor anything else in all creation, will be able to separate us from the love of God in Christ Jesus our Lord.

we recognize that this was the writer's way of pointing to the number of persons.

Although there is a debate about how much Paul was influenced by Greek philosophy and whether he used the language without adopting the current views, most students of Pauline thought judge him to be strongly Jewish. For Paul does not contrast flesh and spirit, but flesh and Spirit. In this chapter he is not describing divisions within a person. He is comparing life oriented around the creature to life which participates in the Spirit. Life in the Spirit is the same thing as being in Christ. The contrast is not between a bad and a good part of a person. It is a comparison between life lived apart from good relationships with God and others and life which relates faithfully to God and to God's creation.

Paul's way of speaking of life in the Spirit is sometimes named a faith or Christ mysticism, one which involves a trustful stance toward God. This is different from mysticism which implies the experience of complete identity with the divine. To have one's mind set on the flesh is to determine that one can live apart from God. To have one's gaze focused on the glory and Way of God is to live as one who is led by the Spirit. To live according to the flesh is to desire to please self. To be led by the Spirit is to strive to please God. According to Paul, spiritual is not the opposite of material. Rather, spiritual refers to right use of and harmonious relationships with the material.

This may seem very theoretical and theological. But it does make a difference in how we live in relation to some basic issues. We will consider here two such issues: attitudes toward sex and sexuality and attitudes toward politics.

We live in a culture which features and exploits sex in such a way that it is helpful for Christians, from time to time, to restate a Christian perspective. Historically, there has been a predominant outlook derived from one kind of flesh-spirit dualism. This is the belief that "the passions of the flesh" are basically evil and need to be repressed, held in check, or at best tolerated by the higher spiritual nature of a person. Some medieval and Puritan Christians supported the doctrine of original sin from the observation that each person is conceived through lustful sexual relationships. In reaction to this view that sex is basically bad, the current popular mood seems to assume that sex is basically natural and therefore good, regardless of how we go about it. Doing what comes naturally, with whomever and whenever we desire, seems to be the popular message.

Pauline dualism, a dualism of basic orientation rather than one of divisions within a person, will not accept either of the above positions. Sex is neither basically bad nor independently good. Sexual relationships are sacred if they are in the context of a covenant of mutual commitment and concern for one another and the glory of God. Sexual activity can be fleshly if engaged in without basic respect and concern for others and the desire to do the will of God.

Similarly, the different kinds of dualism can be applied to the attitude Christians take toward politics. It has often been said that the church should stay out of politics and stick to its business of saving souls. But if a soul refers to the total person, then anything which helps a total person come into proper relationship with God, others, and creation is a part of the business of the church.

Some people maintain that the nuclear arms race is a political issue and not a spiritual question. As generally understood, however, the political encompasses concerns for peace and justice as well as for government, laws, and wars. As Christians, we know that the biblical visions about the kingdom of God intersect with the above concerns at many points. To be political can indeed be sinful and represent life in the flesh if such action is not committed to God's glory and the neighbor's good. Interest in peace and justice can be spiritual, however, when such concerns are rooted in discipleship to the Lord of history.

An additional point about Paul's flesh-Spirit dualism may be helpful. It is the way Paul defines death: "To set the mind on the flesh is death, but to set the mind on the Spirit is life and peace" (Rom. 8:6). In our common usage, death refers to the end of our physical existence. But Paul is more holistic. Death also occurs when we cut off relationships with others and with God. In the New Testament, eternal life begins now. The same is true of death. When persons have an entirely wrong orientation, one focused on self and alienated from the universe, death becomes a present reality. This New Testament understanding of death may help shed light on the mystery of the unpardonable sin against the Holy Spirit (Matt. 12:31). To completely separate oneself from the love of God and right relationships with others would mean a state of death which would make it impossible to be accepted and forgiven.

Theologia Gloriae and Theologia Crucis

"I consider that the sufferings of this present time are not worth comparing with the glory that is to be revealed to us" (Rom. 8:18). Interpreters of Romans 8 often note how Paul relates suffering to the theme of glory. Traditionally, this contrast between suffering and splendor has been known as one between a theology of glory and a theology of the cross.

These two kinds of theologies have a long history in Christian life and thought. Theologies of glory center on the majesty, power, sovereignty, and ultimate victory of God. Theologies of the cross focus on the patience, meekness, and suffering love of God. A theology of glory looks toward the empty tomb and the triumph of the Easter story. A theology of the cross points to Christ's passion, suffering and crucifixion. From the human side, a theology of glory looks to what God can do for us to help us through life and grant us assurance of a future life in heaven. A theology of the cross calls us to participate in God's suffering for the sins of the world. A theology of glory is a theology of success: Families who pray together stay together. A theology of the cross leads us in that narrow way where few enter and calls us to count the cost we will have to pay because of our nonconformity to this fallen world.

Theologies of Glory

Obviously, we live in a day in which there is a revival of theologies of glory. Charismatic movements, voices of the electronic church, and much popular literature have been sharing with us something of the joy, new life, power, and sense of victory which is available through a Spirit-filled life personally related to Jesus Christ. A major theme in Romans 8 says the same: "The sufferings of this present time are not

153

worth comparing with the glory that is to be revealed to us. . . . The Spirit helps us in our weakness. . . . We know that in everything God works for good. . . . If God is for us, who is against us?'' Nothing ''will be able to separate us from the love of God in Christ Jesus our Lord'' (vv. 18, 26, 28, 31, 39).

Our Anabaptist side too often has focused on our need to suffer without pointing to the joy and victory of the faith. Our emphasis on discipleship needs a strong dose of the assurance which permeates this eighth chapter of Romans. We have rightly emphasized the theme of service. But we also must know personally what it means ''to have received the spirit of sonship'' (v. 15). In Roman practice an adopted child was by no means a second-class person. Roman emperors would adopt young boys and appoint them as their successors. Many in our tradition need the power and joy which comes through the assurance of the witness of the Spirit that we are truly children of God (v. 16). This is not just good news for us. It is the good news to be proclaimed as a part of our evangelistic message.

There are real dangers to theologies of glory, however, when they are separated from the theology of the cross. This becomes apparent as we consider where people look to find manifestations of God's Spirit. Our human tendency is to want to look for the presence of God in situations of majesty and success. If we had been in charge, we would have had God coming as a king, riding on a beautiful white horse, and residing in a dazzling castle. Instead, God sent a baby born in a stinking barn to a lowly handmaiden.

Martin Luther made this same point through a personal story. On Good Friday he was in his chamber contemplating how Christ suffered for us when a bright vision appeared on the wall. The Savior Christ with five wounds was looking at him. He reflected: ''I thought first that here was a heavenly vision, but the more I thought, I felt that it was a juggling of the devil. For Christ appeared in His word in a more crude and humble form'' (Luther's *Table-Talk*, quoted in H. T. Kerr's *A Compend to Luther's Theology*, p. 57). Here Luther was penitent that he had wanted something more spectacular than the way God did it.

The same is true today. Though there is good in Christian talk shows on religious television, they can be misleading. They may lead us to see the Spirit's presence more clearly in a famous singer who makes millions from religious records than in a person who has spent many years in jail for participating in human rights struggles. We may see the presence of the Spirit more in the success stories of celebrities than in the common service of humble Christians nearby. We may come to identify the presence of the Spirit more with those who dress in the latest fashions than with those who wear the clothes of the world's poor. We can be led to look for God's power only in what God does for us instead of discerning God's presence in the sufferings of those who are treated unjustly.

Theology of the Cross

In Romans 12, as in the epistle of 1 Corinthians, Paul does not neglect the theology of the cross. Scholars agree that Paul, in writing to the Corinthians, was dealing with a congregation which was high on the Spirit. Paul's letter shares joyfully with the Corinthians about the gifts of the Spirit; yet he begins the letter with a strong dose of the theology of the cross. Featuring the foolishness of the cross, he writes that God chose what is weak, foolish, lowly, and despised in the world in order that no human might boast in the presence of God. In 1 Corinthians 4, Paul chides the people for boasting about being filled with the Spirit and acting like kings. He proceeds to contrast their wise and strong appearance with his own weak and persecuted status. He suggests that they, too, should exemplify the way of the cross.

A current pitfall of some in the Spirit movement is to want to eliminate too quickly and too easily the notion of suffering for the Christian. This is often seen in the one-to-one equation which is made between faith and healing. If you have enough faith, it is promised, you will be healed. The other side of this belief tragically tells others that if they are not healed, it is because they are weak in faith. I have often related my experience with William Beahm, long-time dean at Bethany Seminary. As I visited with him during his bout with terminal cancer, I could clearly see that he had to suffer not only excruciating pain but also the well-meaning but, in reality, cruel admonitions of brothers and sisters who suggested that he did not have sufficient faith. Jesus did promise "Whatever you ask in my name, I will do it" (John 14:14). But to ask in the name of Jesus is to be in the spirit of the One who prayed, "Nevertheless not as I will, but as thou wilt" (Matt. 26:39).

Though Romans 8 is a great example of a biblical theology of glory, it also contains some important accents on a theology of the cross. The kind of suffering which we endure as joint heirs with Christ (v. 17) must be distinguished from the trials that impinge on everyone as human beings. Thus, Paul is not referring to sickness, accidents, or death of a loved person, as important as these are to us in our community of love and concern. Rather, Paul is here referring to

156

the suffering which comes as a result of following Jesus. There is human suffering which comes from a lack of faith. There is also suffering which may be the fruit of faithfulness. And to make it all the more puzzling, there is human suffering which is unrelated to our virtue or lack of virtue. It comes, like God's rain, on the just and on the unjust.

Paul touches on this theme in a fascinating passage on the suffering of the entire creation (Rom. 8:8-18). He borrows language from the pangs of childbirth as he speaks of the groaning and suffering of all creation which precedes and participates in the coming of the new age. In Genesis 3:17 the universe was cursed because of the fall of Adam and Eve. The same is true today. Human beings are responsible for the pollution of our air and streams, for the gross misuse of God's good creation for purposes of death instead of life. An almost unimaginable blasphemy against God's creation would occur through nuclear devastation, leaving the good earth dominated by large bugs. Paul suggests, however, that if the sons and daughters of God are saved, through them the universe itself might be redeemed.

In spite of this important relationship between people, the creatures, and the rest of creation, there remains the mystery of earthquakes, cyclones, tornadoes, floods, and other disasters which are not related to the good or evil of human beings. We also place these natural disasters in God's providential hands, trusting that all things will ultimately work for good.

For Paul, Christian hope is not hope which turns its back on the reality of evil. In 2 Corinthians 11:24-28 he writes that being joined to Christ does not make life any easier. Often, it is quite the opposite. But Christians can still take courage both from the prospect of glory and from assistance already given them by the Holy Spirit. The passages which suggest predestination can only be understood in the context of Christian assurance and hope. At the center of Paul's thought is the affirmation that God's goodness is amazing and undeserved, that we can rejoice in the midst of adversity because of our confidence in God's promises.

"If God be for us, who is against us?" Such an affirmation could be but another expression of cheap grace, of singing the "give-me-God" blues. For Paul, however, this affirmation provides the context for faithful witness. Tribulation, distress, persecution, famine, nakedness, or sword cannot separate us from the love of Christ (Rom. 8:35).

Recently a group of Christians passed out leaflets to a large religious gathering. They were asking people to decide for the World Peace Pledge: "In the light of my faith in God I am prepared to live without nuclear weapons in my country." The group experienced a great amount of hostility as many expressed fear of the Soviet Union. "How can we trust the Russians?" they yelled. Though attending a conservative rally, they were not ready to confess, "If God be for us, who is against us?"

Security is to be found in God, not at all in military strength. May we all know something of the inseparable love of God which casts out fear, including the fear of the Russians. May our lives express these great Pauline messages of faith, hope, and trust in the love of Christ.

Both a Theology of Glory and of the Cross

In conclusion, you might guess that anyone who teaches theology will say that we need both a theology of glory and a theology of the cross. We need to discern the Spirit in God's majesty, God's healing, and in our participation in the first fruits of the kingdom. But we also need to discern the Spirit of God in humble, lowly, painful, and unexpected places. We need to be grateful to God without attempting to manipulate the Spirit for our own purposes. Any theology of the cross without a theology of glory will mean that we grit our teeth when we preach, when we suffer, and when we are persecuted. For we will not know the message and manifestation of Christian joy, power, and victory. But a theology of glory without a theology of the cross is tempted to bask in the Spirit in order to escape the problems of this world. The Spirit of power, grace, and victory does not separate us from but comes in the midst of life's problems, sufferings, and sins.

In the words of the song, we cannot wear the crown if we do not bear the cross. Now, if you have not read it, read Romans 8. And if you have, read it again.

Bibliography

Biblical Authority and Inspiration

Biblical Interpretation in the Life of the Church. Scottdale: Mennonite Publishing House, 1976. Study guide to a 1975 study report of the Mennonite Church General Assembly.

Brown, Dale W. "Inner and Outer Word: The View of the Bible." In *Understanding Pietism.* Grand Rapids: William B. Eerdmans Publishing Company, 1978.

Deeter, Joan, *Biblical Inspiration and Authority: A Study Guide to the 1979 Annual Conference Paper.* Elgin: The Brethren Press, 1980.

Durnbaugh, Donald. "Brethren and the Authority of the Scriptures." *Brethren Life and Thought* 13 (Summer 1968): 170-183.

Schrag, Martin. "The Early Brethren Concept of Authority." *Brethren Life and Thought* 9 (Autumn 1964): 109-126.

Wenger, J. C. *God's Word Written.* Scottdale: Herald Press, 1966.

Yoder, John H. "The Hermeneutics of the Anabaptists." *Mennonite Quarterly Review* 41 (Oct. 1967): 291-308.

Doctrine of the Holy Spirit

Baer, Richard, Jr. "Quaker Silence, Catholic Liturgy, and Pentecostal Glossolalia." In *Perspectives on the New Pentecostalism.* Russell P. Spittler. Grand Rapids: Baker Book House, 1976.

Brown, Dale W. *Flamed by the Spirit: Biblical Definitions of the Holy Spirit, A Brethren Perspective.* Elgin: The Brethren Press, 1978.

159

Brunk, George R., ed. *Encounter with the Holy Spirit.* Grand Rapids: William B. Eerdmans Publishing Company, 1975.

Carter, Charles. *The Person and Ministry of the Holy Spirit: A Wesleyan Perspective.* Grand Rapids: Baker Book House, 1974.

Green, Michael. *I Believe in the Holy Spirit.* Grand Rapids: William B. Eerdmans Publishing Company, 1975.

Hoffman, Jasper. *The Holy Spirit.* Marion, IN: Wesley Press, 1944.

Loane, Marcus L. *The Hope of Glory: An Exposition of the Eighth Chapter in the Epistle to the Romans.* Waco: Word, 1968.

Montague, George T. *The Holy Spirit: Growth of a Biblical Tradition. Ramsey, NJ: Paulist Press, 1976.*

Stott, John R. W. *Baptism and Fullness.* Downers Grove: Inter-Varsity Press, 1976.

Good Interpretations of Anabaptism for Teachers

Friedmann, Robert. *The Theology of Anabaptism.* Scottdale: Herald Press, 1973.

Klaassen, Walter, ed. *Anabaptism in Outline.* Scottdale: Herald Press, 1981.

Sections on Faith in Denominational Histories

Durnbaugh, Donald F., ed. *The Church of the Brethren Past and Present.* Elgin: The Brethren Press, 1971. Vernard Eller's chapter on "Beliefs."

Pannabecker, Samuel F. *Open Doors: A History of the General Conference Church.* Newton: Faith and Life Press, 1975. Chapter 15, "Holding the Faith."

Toews, John A. *A History of the Mennonite Brethren Church: Pilgrims and Pioneers.* Fresno: Board of Christian Ministries, 1975. See section on "Faith in Ferment."

Wenger, J. C. *Mennonite Church in America.* Scottdale: Herald Press, 1966. See chapter 13, "Major Features of Anabaptist-Mennonite Theology" and "Mennonite Confession of Faith, 1963," in Appendices.

Wittlinger, Carlton O. *Quest for Piety and Obedience: The Story of the Brethren in Christ.* Nappanee, IN: Evangel Press, 1978.

Federal communicator commlolo
1919 M. Street, Washington D, C